Exploring Matthew

Everyday Stories

Exploring Matthew

Everyday Stories

Book 2
Chapters 15 – 28

– a Bible study and preaching resource

Al W. Adams

LUCAS
PARK
BOOKS

ST. LOUIS, MISSOURI

Table of Contents

Jesus Teaches About God's Coming Kingdom (24:1 – 25:46)

Jesus Dies and is Raised to Life! (26:1 – 28:20)

Introduction and Welcome!

Bible. Study. These are two words which many (maybe even you) have not been too enthusiastic about. For many, the word 'Bible' is connected with rules and restrictions. Not just that, but what could it possibly have to do with life today? Written thousands of years ago, hasn't it lost its relevance? In a word, no.

And what about the word 'study'? Now there's an exciting word (not)! Let's see, how about the image of long boring hours spent learning things you'll never need? Didn't you leave all that behind when you got out of school?

I want you to try on some new words: experience, explore, and everyday. Let's call them the 'three e's'. What would it be like to experience the Bible texts in your life, right here and now? How about exploring the stories in the setting of your everyday world?

The Exploring...Everyday Stories Bible experience series seeks to help you do just that. You may be someone who has never read the Bible. Maybe you don't even own one! Perhaps you've been in and out of churches all your life, but you've never really connected 'The Book' to your real everyday life. If so, then welcome to the Bible in 'three e's'!

This series is designed to be experienced individually or in groups who are sharing the exploration together. All the Scripture passages are printed in this book, so if you don't own a Bible or yours is hard for you to understand, wait a bit before you purchase one.

You will experience four Bible translations/versions in this exploration journey: (1) The New Revised Standard Version; (2) The New Living Translation; (3) The Contemporary English Version; and (4) The Message Version. Each is described in Appendix 1 of this book along with a purchasing source should you decide to buy one or more of them.

In each chapter, you will read a section of Scripture. Most times, it will be presented in two or more translations/versions, so you can experience the 'flavor' of each. Then you will read a true (unless otherwise noted) 'everyday' story related to the Scripture, followed by a connection between the Bible passage and the story. Finally, reflection questions are presented to guide you in further thought and exploration.

Like many of you, I came to a place in my own life where I wondered about the relevance of the Bible to my real, everyday life. Then my eyes were opened as God led me to connect things going on in everyday life with Bible texts. It is my hope and prayer that this exploration experience will lead you to new excitement and growth in your spiritual life. May God richly bless your explorations, may you experience the Holy Spirit in new and powerful ways, and may your eyes be opened to the real presence of Christ in your everyday life!

Rev. Dr. Al W. Adams

1

Heart Check-Up

Then the disciples approached and said to him, "Do you know that the Pharisees took offense when they heard what you said?" He answered, "Every plant that my heavenly father has not planted will be uprooted. Let them alone; they are blind guides of the blind. And if one blind person guides another, both will fall into a pit."

*But Peter said to him, "Explain this parable to us." Then he said, "Are you also still without understanding? Do you not see that whatever goes into the mouth enters the stomach, and goes out into the sewer? But what comes out of the mouth proceeds from **the heart, and this is what defiles. For out of the heart come evil intentions**, murder, adultery, fornication, theft, false witness, slander. **These are what defile a person**, but to eat with unwashed hands does not defile."*

- Matthew 15: 12-20 (New Revised Standard Version)

Then his disciples came over to him and asked, "Do you know that you insulted the Pharisees by what you said?" Jesus answered, "Every plant that my father in heaven did not plant will be pulled up by the roots. Stay away from those Pharisees! They are like blind people leading other blind people, and all of them will fall into a ditch."

Peter replied, "What did you mean when you talked about the things that make people unclean?"

*Jesus then said, "Don't any of you know what I am talking about by now? Don't you know that the food that you put into your mouth goes into your stomach and then out of your body? But **the words that come out of your mouth come from your heart. And they are what make you unfit to worship God.** Out of your heart come evil thoughts, murder, unfaithfulness in marriage, vulgar deeds, stealing, telling lies, and insulting others. **These are what make you unclean.** Eating without washing your hands will not make you unfit to worship God."*

- Matthew 15: 12-20 (Contemporary English Version)

* * * * * * * * * *

The dirt had been there so long it was a part of his hands, his feet, his face. Arriving by ambulance, he was whisked into the emergency department, already hooked up to heart monitors and an IV. He'd **said his name was Bill, just Bill.** The way most staff members walked by him in the hall on his gurney, you'd have thought he had some highly contagious alien disease. Not so. Bill had just been living in the park, train and bus stations - wherever he could – for the last 20 years.

Oh, but his eyes – they sparkled. How could that be? Like sapphires in his face, they glowed with life. In a seemingly worn out, dirty body, those eyes didn't miss a beat. **His case fell to a young doctor**, new to the emergency department. The doctor cautiously approached and greeted Bill, who smiled back. **"Yea, guess I'm a pretty dangerous character. Sure you wanta get this close?"** Bill chuckled. The young doctor started to back up,

1

then resolutely held his ground. He listened to Bill's heart and read his test results. "Sir...." Bill's eyes lit up, then misted over. **"You called me 'sir'. Nobody's done that in a long time."** The doctor, anxious to get Bill to a test he really needed, continued. **"Well, sir, we've got to get you up for a cardiac catheterization.** That's a test where they......." Bill interrupted. "You know, I **was a medic at Normandy.** I follow all that medical stuff. That bad, huh? Well, let's get it done."

The young doctor got to know Bill as he remained on the gurney in the hall for over an hour waiting for a room (even though there were rooms available). The young doctor was at first confused about this, then angry as three hours went by with no call from the cardiac lab. Bill's heart condition had deteriorated steadily since his arrival. **Finally he understood what Bill had known all along. The ingrained dirt in Bills' hands and face, his outside appearance – destined him to be last in line.**

The doctor stopped to see Bill more and more often, frustrated that he couldn't do more. **The sparkle in Bill's eyes never wavered.** He came by to let Bill know he was going to grab a bite in the hospital cafeteria, but he'd be back within an hour. It was then that Bill said something he'd never forget.

"Doctor?" he moved closer so he could hear Bill, as his voice was growing weaker. **"Doctor, I see you washing your hands all the time.Keep your heart clean like that too. You can live without your hands, but you can't live without your heart. Don't let them, what they're doing to me, don't let it dirty your heart. Got that?"**

"Yes sir, I do. But I wish.....it makes me so angry...."
"Don't let them dirty your heart. Do I hafta tell you again?"
"No sir, I got it. I'll be right back."

Just45 minutes later, he returned from the cafeteria to find Bill's spot in the hall empty.
"Oh, the street guy? He died right after you left." The desk person was surprised at the sorrow on the young doctor's face – and the anger. "Oh, please. He was just a street guy. Here." And she handed him another patient chart.

Right then, **Bill's lesson sunk in as he looked her in the eye.** No sparkle. No shine. What he saw was.... a dirty heart. *What a waste,* he thought, as he walked away. She could have made such a difference.

No one could be found to claim Bill's body, so the doctor and his wife did. His wife researched Bill and found his last name and military record. They made sure Bill received the honor his clear heart deserved. **"That day, I got the biggest 'heart check-up' of my entire life.", he said at Bill's funeral as he told this story, "And I want to be like Bill – I want a clean heart, just like his."**

* * * * * * * * *

So, how's your heart? Due for a check up? Right here, right now. Check it out. Spend some time with God. Listen again to Jesus:

"But the words that come out of your mouth come from your heart. And they are what make you unfit to worship God."

You see, if our hearts are dirty,we need a heart check-up. We need to come to God, confessing our need for healing, for cleansing. **We gather dirt and grime just in our daily living.** Our times spent alone with God, sharing Jesus' Table, and in Christian community all work together to clean and shine our hearts for clean-heart living. **Our worship time empowers us to go out into the world again, glowing and sparkling –** just like Bill. Just like him, we can serve and share until our last breath here on earth, and when we meet God face to face, we'll hear, "Well done, good and faithful servant!", and **we'll see the eternal clear sparkle in God's eyes.**

Reflections

Have you ever felt 'last in line', like Bill? What was it like? How did you respond?

Do you wish you'd responded differently? Why or why not?

When you hear the words, "Heart Check-Up", what do you think of?

What would you expect to happen if Jesus gave you a "Heart Check-Up?"

2

Crumbs of Faith

Jesus then left Galilee and went north to the region of Tyre and Sidon. A Gentile woman who lived there came to him, pleading, "Have mercy on me, Lord, Son of David! For my daughter has a demon in her, and it is severely tormenting her."

But Jesus gave her no reply – not even a word. Then his disciples urged him to send her away. **"Tell her to leave, they said, "She is bothering us with all her begging."**

Then he said to the woman, "I was sent only to help the people of Israel – God's lost sheep – not the Gentiles."

But she came and worshiped him and pleaded again, "Lord, help me!" "It isn't right to take food from the children and throw it to the dogs," he said.

"Yes, Lord," she replies, "but even dogs are permitted to eat crumbs that fall beneath their master's table."

"Woman," Jesus said to her, your faith is great. Your request is granted." And her daughter was instantly healed.

Jesus returned to the Sea of Galilee and climbed a hill and sat down. A vast crowd **brought him the lame, blind, cripples, mute, and many others with physical difficulties, and they laid them before Jesus. And he healed them all.** *The crowd was amazed! Those who hadn't been able to speak were talking, the crippled were made well, the lame were walking around, and those who had been blind could see again!* **And they praised the God of Israel.**

- Matthew 15: 21-31 (New Living Translation)

From there Jesus took a trip to Tyre and Sidon. They had hardly arrived when aCanaanite woman came down from the hills and pleaded, "Mercy, Master, Son of David! My daughter is cruelly afflicted by an evil spirit."

Jesus ignored her. **The disciples came to him and complained, "Now she's bothering us. Would you please take care of her? She's driving us crazy."**

Jesus refused, telling them, "I've got my hands full dealing with the lost sheep of Israel."

Then the woman came back to Jesus, went to her knees, and begged, "Master, help me." He said, "It's not right to take bread out of children's mouths and throw it to the dogs."

She was quick: **"You're right, Master, but beggar dogs do get scraps from the Master's table."**

Jesus gave in. "Oh, woman, **your faith is something else.** *What you want is what you get. Right then her daughter became well.*

After Jesus returned, he walked along Lake Galilee and then climbed a mountain and took his place, ready to receive visitors. They came, tons of them, bringing along the paraplegic, the blind, the maimed, the mute – **all sorts of people in need – and more or less threw them down at Jesus' feet to see what he would do with them. He healed them.** *When the people saw the mutes speaking, the maimed healthy, the paraplegics walking around, the blind looking around, they were astonished and let everyone know that* **God was blazingly alive among them.**

- Matthew 15: 21-31 (The Message Version)

* * * * * * * * *

"Can I have these?" Todd looked up from his desk. He was so busy grading the last of the reading tests, he hadn't even noticed the small boy enter his classroom. His room was right by the back doors of the school, and many times kids would come in to use the bathroom or get a drink after school as they played on the playground right outside.

"Mister teacher, can I please have these?" Todd had never seen this boy before. Where did he come from? Why was he digging through the trash can? Todd had just cleaned out his files and the shelves, getting ready for the summer. Old worn paperback books, old worksheets, pencils, whatever – it had all gone in the trash. What could this youngster possibly want with any if that? Surely he too was ready for a break from school?

"Hey, teacher, you speak English? I said, CAN I HAVE THESE.....PLEASE?"
Todd, embarrassed, finally realized he hadn't answered the boy!
"Well, they're left from the boys and girls in my class...."
The boy put the books and papers back. As he turned to go, he looked back over his shoulder at Todd. "Yes sir, that's what my mom told me. She said, 'School's not for you. We don't have money for clothes and books and all that stuff.'"

Todd was too stunned to answer. The boy turned away, then suddenly straightened up and turned, a steely glint in his young eyes. "Even poor kids need to read. Even me. This is your trash, but it's mine now. It's not trash to me."

Realization struck Todd like a lightning bolt. This boy wasn't trash! No way!
"Hey, wait a minute. I'm Todd. What's your name? How'd you like to help me move some stuff? Why, you could earn a whole bunch of books and neat stuff! Lots of us teachers could use help from a great guy like you – how about it?"

That's how it started. And it didn't end, even after 'little' Jay wasn't so little any more. Not even after Todd and a few of the other teachers got together and decided to take Jay and his two sisters under their wing. Not after all of them graduated from high school. Not even after Todd retired. Todd and two of the other teachers attended every graduation. They were there when Jay graduated from college too, and Todd helped Jay set up his first classroom – right down the hall from his old room.

Todd learned an important lesson the day he met Jay. God called him as a teacher. Not just a teacher of a select group of kids. Not just in that room. Not just for nine months of the year. No. God called Todd to be a beacon for Jesus Christ, to use his gifts to touch lives – all the lives God entrusted him with. Even after school. Even when school was out. Even with kids digging through the trash, thinking themselves unworthy of the education and care other kids received. Todd learned there was no 'not good enough', no 'unworthy' with God. With God, there was just grace, just love – for all.

* * * * * * * * *

I think Jesus learned something that day. I wonder if He too wanted the woman to leave. He doesn't say that. He doesn't say anything. How could He miss her though? She was so persistent that she was 'bothering us', 'driving us crazy' from the disciples' viewpoint.

And then what? When she finally gets the Master's attention (or at least gets an answer), he tells her **she's not good enough?! Can't you just see her beginning to turn away?** Can't you just see her mind whirling? Can it be that she came all this way, risked coming here – only to be turned down? Why, this **was about her daughter, her little girl!** Her first reaction could justifiably have been anger – He had called her and her family....dogs!!

But **she'd come all this way, so what now?** Then a thought struck her! Why, even dogs (not the cute puppy pets we have today, but usually wild, scavenger types) got leftovers! **Jesus' leftovers would be fine**, why as powerful as He was, that's all it would take. She was sure of it!

So **she challenged Jesus.** Did you catch that? She challenged....God! Listen to the **amazing answer:**
*"Woman," Jesus said to her, **your faith is great. Your request is granted."** And her daughter was instantly healed.*

You might be tempted to think this was the end of the story – but read on. Can't you just see Jesus thinking on this encounter as He travels back to the Sea of Galilee? **What does He do next?**

Scripture tells us that, *"They came, tons of them, bringing along the paraplegic, the blind, the maimed, the mute – all sorts of people in need – and more or less threw them down at Jesus' feet to see what he would do with them. He healed them."*

Not just 'lost sheep of Israel'. Crowds. Tons. All kinds.
That's right. Jesus came for – all of us.
For Todd. For Jay. For his two sisters.
For you. Even on your worst, most unworthy-feeling, unlovable-seeming day.
For you.
Think about it. Spread the Word.

Reflections

How hard is it to claim the fact the Jesus came...for YOU?

How can you, like Todd, use your uniqueness to serve as a beacon for Christ?

Could you, like the woman in Scripture, challenge God to show you how that might be? Are you ready for the answer – ready to listen and put it into action?

3

Leftovers

Then Jesus called his disciples to him and said, "I feel sorry for these people. They have been here with me for three days, and they have nothing left to eat. I don't want to send them away hungry, or they will faint along the road."

The disciples replied, "And where would we get enough food out here in the wilderness for all of them to eat?"

Jesus asked, "How many loaves of bread do you have?" They replied, "Seven, and a few small fish."

So Jesus told all the people to sit down on the ground. Then he took the seven loaves and the fish, thanked God for them, broke them into pieces, and gave them to the disciples, who distributed the food to the crowd.

They all ate until they were full, and **when the scraps were picked up,** *there were* **seven large baskets of food left over!** *There were four thousand men who were fed that day, in addition to all the women and children.*

Then Jesus sent the people home, and he got into a boat and crossed over to the region of Magadan.

(Matthew 15: 32-39 – New Living Translation)

Then Jesus called his disciples to him and said, "I have compassion for the crowd, because they have been with me now for three days and have nothing to eat; and I do not want to send them away hungry, for they might faint on the way."

The disciples said to him, "Where are we to get enough bread in the desert to feed so great a crowd?"

Jesus asked them, "How many loaves have you?" They said, "Seven, and a few small fish."

Then ordering the crowd to sit down on the ground, he took the seven loaves and the fish; and after giving thanks he broke them and gave them to the disciples, and the disciples gave them to the crowds.

And all of them ate and were filled; and **they took up the broken pieces left over, seven baskets full.** *Those who had eaten were four thousand men, besides women and children.*

After sending away the crowds, he got into the boat and went to the region of Magadan.

- Matthew 15: 32-39 (New Revised Standard Version)

* * * * * * * * *

"They leave you out here too? Yeah, they're in there deciding what to do with me. How come you're here?" My boredom and impatience fled. Waiting for my friends to finalize the adoption of their new daughters, it seemed as though I'd been waiting hours. I hadn't even noticed him, and I wondered how long he'd been sitting there. **That's how I met Jonah.**

Jonah had come home from a fun weekend with his best friend to find his entire family gone. Just gone. Jonah told me his parents had been fighting a lot about money; his dad lost his job last month. "But I don't eat much, and I didn't even ask for anything for Christmas..." He was trying to figure it all out.

Jonah said they'd left a note telling him they loved him and he'd have to 'be a man' now (at twelve years old?). His parents had taken his four little sisters and brothers, but Jonah said maybe it was because teenagers were so expensive. He'd overheard his mother saying that the night before he'd gone to spend the weekend with his friend. "And I'll be thirteen next month." Jonah mumbled, looking down, **"I guess I'm like leftovers. When they get too old, you just throw them out."**

It was definitely a 'God-thing'. It just popped out of my mouth. "Jesus never throws away leftovers. He gathers them up."

I got the 'yeah, right' look as my reward. So I took that as an invitation, and I shared the stories of Jesus feeding the two crowds, four and five thousand (plus!). And both times – Jesus' disciples were careful to collect the leftovers. Gathered them in fact – in baskets.

I told Jonah about Jesus' first missionary (the crazy guy who lived in the cemetery – Mark 5), the king of all the 'leftover' human beings!

Hope. That's what began to glimmer in Jonah's eyes as we talked. I could just feel God at work. Oh yes, God's power at work in us CAN do far more than we can ask – or even imagine! (see Ephesians 3:20-21)

No one was more surprised than I when, **a year later**, Jonah walked into my science classroom. He'd had a rough year, but he'd found a caring foster family, and he beamed as he shared with me that HIS adoption would be final by the end of the school year. **"My foster parents, they had one of those baskets you told me about that day. They just gathered me up, just like Jesus told those guys to do in the Bible!"**

* * * * * * * * *

Human beings have leftovers. Jesus doesn't.
We throw leftovers away. Jesus refuses to give up. He gathers themup in baskets.

On your bad days, your 'leftover' days, feel yourself gathered up.
Knowyou are precious to God.
Precious enough for God to send Jesus for you. Yes, you.

On your good days, grab a basket. Reach out to the Jonahs you meet.
Be a disciple. Spread eternal hope. You too can help God gather the broken. Just be open to the 'God-incidences' in your life.

Be a disciple. Do it for Jesus, the Christ, your Lord and Savior.

Reflections

What 'leftovers' came to your mind and heart as you read Jonah's story?

What does the statement "Jesus doesn't have leftovers" mean to you?

Knowing that, apply it to the challenge to "be a disciple". How does that change this real-life call for you?

4

Expired!

The Pharisees and Sadducees came to Jesus and tried to test him by asking for a sign from heaven. He told them,
"If the sky is red in the evening, you say the weather will be good. But if the sky is red and gloomy in the morning, you say it is going to rain. You can tell what the weather will be like by looking at the sky. But you don't understand what is happening now. You want a sign because you are evil and won't believe! But the only sign you will be given is what happened to Jonah. Then Jesus left.

*The disciples had forgotten to bring any bread when they crossed the lake. Jesus then warned them, **"Watch out! Guard against the yeast of the Pharisees and Sadducees."***

The disciples talked this over and said to each other, "He must be saying this because we didn't bring along any bread."

*Jesus knew what they were thinkingand said, "You surely don't have much faith! Why are you talking about not having any bread? Don't you understand? Have you forgotten about the five thousand people and **all those baskets of leftovers** from just five loaves of bread? And what about the four thousand people and **all those baskets of leftovers** from only seven loaves of bread? **Don't you know by now that I am not talking to you about bread? Watch out for the yeast of the Pharisees and Sadducees."***

- Matthew 16: 1-12 (Contemporary English Version)

Some Pharisees and Sadducees were on him again, pressing him to prove himself to them. He told them, "You have a saying that goes, 'Red sky at night, sailor's delight; red sky at morning, sailors take warning.' You find it easy enough to forecast the weather – why can't you read the signs of the times? An evil and wanton generation is always wanting signs and wonders. The only sign you'll get is the Jonah sign." Then he turned on his heel and walked away.

*On their way to the other side of the lake, the disciples discovered they had forgotten to bring along bread. In the meantime, Jesus said to them, **"Keep a sharp eye out for Pharisee-Sadducee yeast."***

*Thinking he was scolding them for forgetting bread, they discussed in whispers what to do. Jesus knew what they were doing and said, "Why all these worried whispers about forgetting the bread? Runt believers! Haven't you caught on yet? I you remember the five loaves of bread and the five thousand people, and **how many fragments you picked up?** Or the seven loaves that fed four thousand, and **how many baskets of leftovers you collected?** Haven't you realized yet that **bread isn't the problem? The problem is yeast. Pharisee-Sadducee yeast. Then they got it: that he wasn't concerned about eating, but teaching – the Pharisee-Sadducee kind of teaching.***

- Matthew 16: 1-12 (The Message Version)

* * * * * * * * * *

10

It was perfect. Bob could buy the restaurant of his dreams, for even less than he'd hoped, and **the deal included all the equipment and supplies inventory!** He closed the deal and headed over, new keys in hand, a bounce in his step. He could hardly wait!

Bob opened the doors. Hmmm. Well, it smelled kind of musty, probably because it had been shut up a while. He set about opening the windows and propping open the front and back doors. **A fresh breeze blew through.** Ahh, that's better!

He swept and mopped. Then he systematically went through the place and got rid of all the trash. **Old menus – out. Old dirty plasticware – out. On and on he went,** until before long it was lunchtime. Bob sat back and smiled. **This afternoon he'd put up the new stuff**: new wall and table menus, new tableware, new signs, and last, the new restaurant hours on the front door. **Folks had been stopping by all morning asking when he'd be open, and he'd excitedly told them....next week!!**

Hungry for lunch, Bob headed back to the food supply area. He'd been impressed with all the food supplies the previous owners included in the sale. **There would surely be something** there he could fix up for lunch!

Pizza sounded good. Bob turned one of the ovens on and grabbed a couple of cans from the shelf to make some sauce. It was then his eye wandered to the expiration date on the can he was holding. He **couldn't believe his eyes** – why this stuff expired a year ago! He couldn't serve this! Trusting all the food on the shelves, Bob hadn't ordered much from the supplier. All his advertising was for an opening date....next Monday! He frantically began checking all the cans on the food shelves. All but two were WAY old. Great! He'd have pickles and one can of pimentos. **Somehow, pickle and pimento pizza didn't sound like a very marketable dish!**

Angry and frustrated, Bob called his lifelong friend Jim. Jim, trying to hold back laughter at the thought of pickle and pimento pizza, promised to come right over and help after work. "You know, buddy," he said,"Maybe focusing on all that free food wasn't too bright. I keep thinking about how this restaurant thing is what you've been dreaming of your whole life – and now it's yours! How about that? We'll make it work. **Just throw out all that old stuff! This is a new thing!"**

Bob learned a lesson that day. He learned to focus on his vision, on the bigger things in life, instead of counting the cans on the shelves. Oh, he still counted the cans (and checked those expiration dates!), **but his focus was different – on the 'new thing',** as Jim put it – the lifelong dream coming true in his life!

* * * * * * * * *

You see, like Bob we often focus on 'counting the cans' (what we have, our 'stuff') and lose track of the vision – God's plan unfolding in our lives. This focus problem starts small and pretty soon, just like the 'Pharisee-Sadducee yeast' Jesus warns his followers about, our whole life focus is in the wrong place. Sure, **keeping track of our possessions and concrete aspects of our lives is important, but not of the utmost importance!**

Whatever we make the primary focus of our lives is like the yeast Jesus is teaching about. It grows and takes over our whole lives. The Pharisees and Sadducees lived their lives with rules and regulations at the center. Yes, God was important, but they'd allowed the 'yeast' of rules and regulations to take over, pushing the vision of God and God's kingdom to the dim,dark recesses of their lives.

Jesus reminds them (and us) that they're worrying about the wrong thing! He's already proved to them (twice) that He has the bread thing under control! They are to be learning and growing in faith and ministry, using their gifts to spread the Kingdom Good News!!

So how about us? It's really easy, you know, to gradually let the 'yeast' of wrong life focus grow and multiply in our lives until we lose track of our relationship with God. **Take a minute** (OK, maybe several) to honestly examine your life focus today. **What kind of yeast is working in your life? Is it Pharisee-Sadducee yeast? Or is it Jesus Christ yeast?**

If you look closely, and talk to God about it, **you too might just notice that much of what you thought was good on your life's shelves is really.....expired**! As you clean your shelves, how will you restock them?

It's a continuing, growing experience, this shelf cleaning. I practice it each Sunday morning as I prepare for worship. It has given me new growth, joy, and an ever closer walk with Jesus Christ, my Lord and Savior. **I approach His Table with new and clearer vision each week! Won't you join me?**

Reflections

What does "counting the cans" mean to you – in your life?

What would "Pharisee-Sadduccee yeast" look like in today's world?

How about "Jesus Christ yeast"?

Name some ways you could "clean your shelves" ? How could this happen?

5

Silent Confession

When Jesus arrived in the villages of Caesarea Philippi, he asked his disciples, "What are people saying about who the son of Man is?"

They replied, "Some think he is John the Baptizer, some say Elijah, some Jeremiah or one of the other prophets."

He pressed them, "And how about you? Who do you say I am?"

Simon Peter said, "You're the Christ, the Messiah, the Son of the Living God." *Jesus came back, "God bless You, Simon, son of Jonah! You didn't get that answer out of books or from teachers. My Father in heaven, God himself, let you in on this secret of who I really am. And now I'm going to tell you who you are, really are.* **You are Peter, a rock. This is the rock on which I will put together my church, a church so expansive with energy that not even the gates of hell will be able to keep it out.**

"And that's not all. You will have complete and free access to God's kingdom, keys to open any and every door: no more barriers between heaven and earth, earth and heaven. A yes on earth is a yes in heaven. A no on earth is a no in heaven."

He swore the disciples to secrecy. He made them promise they would tell no one that he was the Messiah.

– Matthew 16: 13-20 (The Message Version)

When Jesus came to the region of Caesarea Philippi, he asked his disciples, "Who do people say that the Son of Man is?"

"Well," they replied, "some say John the Baptist, some say Elijah, and others say Jeremiah or one of the other prophets."

Then he asked them, "Who do you say I am?"

Simon Peter answered, "You are the Messiah, the Son of the living God." *Jesus replied, "You are blessed, Simon son of John, because my Father in heaven has revealed this to you. You did not learn this from any human being.* **Now I say to you that you are Peter, and upon this rock I will build my church, and all the powers of hell will not conquer it.**

And I will give you the keys of the Kingdom of Heaven. Whatever you lock on earth will be locked in heaven, and whatever you open on earth will be opened in heaven."

Then he sternly warned them not to tell anyone that he was the Messiah.

- Matthew 16: 13-20 (New Living Translation)

* * * * * * * * *

It was one of thoseSunday mornings I'll never forget. **I was serving as part of a youth/young adult worship leadership team** that went to different churches on 'special' Sundays or when pastors were on vacation. **Usually**

the church sent an outline of how their service was structured, along with any special instructions. Then we'd start planning the service.

This particular church had informed us the week before that there would **be a special pre-recorded piece** (no PowerPoint® back then!) set to 'Amazing Grace' **right after the sermon time**. So that's what we expected – a cool presentation of Amazing Grace.

But oh, my, when the sermon ended and the invitation to accept Christ as Lord and Savior was given, **what happened next was truly awesome.**

A young man's face was the first picture to appear on the screen in the church. I'd seen that face just that morning! As the Amazing Grace tape played, scenes flashed on the screen: baby pictures, school pictures, a picture of two graves (his parents'), pictures of the same young man – homeless with a shopping cart, pictures of him earning his college degree, and finally a picture of him in his classroom teaching. The picture faded to black – for just a second.

Then Brett came back on the screen as the music played on softly in the background. Matthew 16: 13-20 (the Scripture above) rolled across one side of the screen as Brett shared it on the other side in sign language.

Ah, there he is! **I saw him in the second row.** How neat, I thought – he knows sign language so well! The tape ended and Brett came forward with a friend. **It was then I realized he was deaf and could not speak** (audibly anyway). As he signed, his friend translated....

"I used to think God wouldn't want me because I couldn't talk, couldn't hear," he began. "But then I found this Scripture and others like it and I **realized Jesus needed me**." A big smile crossed his face, and laughter bubbled in his friend's eyes. I could tell they'd known each other a long time. "You see, I have to SHOW people Jesus. Most people don't know the language I speak, and I can't speak theirs. **But something amazing happened the other day in my classroom.** One of my students came up to me after class and told me, he said....." Tears started to leak out the corners of Brett's eyes. "He called me his 'rock', said he'd be graduating because of me. His rock.....and even after all those years away from Jesus, away from church, I remembered Peter, the 'rock'."

Brett drew a deep breath. "So I'm here to say **Jesus DOES need me – and you – to be rocks,** to show people the Good News. **I'm here to claim Jesus as my Lord because, well, God's grace is simply....amazing!** And you know what? The powers of hell – I've seen them, and they CAN'T prevail against the Body of Christ. I'm ready to show 'em Jesus. How about you?"

The church was dead silent for about three seconds. Then people slowly began to clap. As the applause grew to a crescendo (there were about 200 folks there), the people rose to their feet.

We played Amazing Grace again. The singing was sweet and oh, so powerful, but the most powerful thing about it happened when Brett and his friend stepped up onto the platform in front of the church (where they could feel the beat and read the words with us) and Brett signed the words as we <u>all</u> sang together.

Simon Peter said, "You're the Christ, the Messiah, the Son of the Living God."
...You are Peter, a rock. This is the rock on which I will put together my church, a church so expansive with energy that not even the gates of hell will be able to keep it out.
...He swore the disciples to secrecy. He made them promise they would tell no one that he was the Messiah.

So what do we say to Brett's challenge: "I'm ready to show 'em Jesus. How about you?"

How ABOUT us?

Reflections

How would you describe the "powers of Hell" in our world today?

In your community? Your life?

How would you describe someone living as a "rock" for Christ in the midst of all that?

Name some ways we can serve as "rocks", loosing the power of Christ into our world and lives.

6

Do WHAT?

(*Remember verse 20: "Then* **he sternly warned them not to tell anyone that he was the Messiah."**)

From that time on, **Jesus began to show his disciples that he must go to Jerusalem and undergo great suffering at the hands of the elders and chief priests and scribes, and be killed, and on the third day be raised.**

And Peter took him aside and began to rebuke him, saying, "God forbid it, Lord! This must never happen to you."

But he turned and said to Peter, "Get behind me, Satan! You are a stumbling block to me; for you are setting your mind not on divine things but on human things."

Then Jesus told his disciples, **"If any want to become my followers, let them deny themselves and take up their cross and follow me.** *For those who want to save their life will lose it, and those who lose their life for my sake will find it. For what will it profit them if they gain the whole world but forfeit their life? Or what will they give in return for their life?*

"For the Son of Man is to come with his angels in the glory of his Father, and then he will repay everyone for what has been done. Truly I tell you, there are some standing here who will not taste death before they see the Son of Man coming in his kingdom."

- Matthew 16: 21-28 (New Revised Standard Version)

(*Remember verse 20:* **"Jesus told his disciples not to tell anyone that he was the Messiah."**)

From then on, Jesus began telling his disciples what would happen to him, He said, **"I must go to Jerusalem. There the nation's leaders, the chief priests, and the teachers of the Law of Moses will make me suffer terribly. I will be killed, but three days later I will rise to life."**

Peter took Jesus aside and told him to stop talking like that. He said, "God would never let this happen to you, Lord!"

Jesus turned to Peter and said, "Satan, get away from me! You're in my way because you think like everyone else and not like God."

Then Jesus said to his disciples, **"If any of you want to be my followers, you must forget about yourself. You must take up your cross and follow me.** *If you want to save your life, you will destroy it. But if you give up your life for me, you will find it. What will you gain, if you own the whole world but destroy yourself? What would you give to get back your soul?*

"The Son of Man will soon come inthe glory of his Father and with his angels to reward all people for what they have done. I promise that some of those standing here will not die before they see the Son of Man coming with his kingdom."

- Matthew 16: 21-28 (Contemporary English Version)

* * * * * * * * * *

Let's look at the sequence here:
Don't tell.
By the way, they're gonna torture and kill me.
Oh, yes, and grab your cross and follow me...
What?

Yep, kind of like that.

Oneevening, asI settled in at our local Starbucks for some reading amid the game night we sponsored, **I noticed a man at the table next to mine, laptop open**, headset on, eyes fixed to the screen, tapping his foot....and crying.

So, OK, I was curious. What was he playing that made him cry? I got up and walked across the room to take a peek. Lyrics. He had lyrics on the screen. At a glance, they looked familiar. He saw me looking, took an earphone out, and asked, **"So, you like Casting Crowns too? Ever heard this one? Wish I'd heard it sooner."**

That's how I met Mike.

Don't tell.
By the way, they're gonna torture and kill me.
Oh, yes, and grab your cross and follow me...
What?

We spent an hour talking about those lyrics. "I figure I got stuck in the 'don't tell' mode", he told me. "Afraid of the consequences of talking about it. My faith, I mean. Never got to the cross-carrying part. Lost my job. My wife. Yeah, she told me it was OK to be a Christian on the weekend. Well, maybe on Sunday, but it'd get me in trouble the rest of the week. So I guess I just chose to hear the 'don't tell' part of what Jesus said."

OK, I got that, but I still didn't get the connection with the song he was playing – not until he invited me to listen and read with him (*American Dream*, by Casting Crowns):

All work and no play may have made Jack a dull boy –
But all work and no God has left Jack with a lost soul.
But he's moving on at full steam.
He's chasing the American dream, and he's gonna give his family the finer things.

Not this time son, I've no time to waste.
Maybe tomorrow we'll have time to play.
And then he slips into his new BMW, and drives farther and farther away.

So he works all day and tries to sleep at night.
He says things will get better; better in time.

'Cause he works and he builds with his own two hands
and he pours all he has in a castle made with sand.
But the wind and the rain are comin' crashing in.
Time will tell just how long his kingdom stands...his kingdom stands.

His American dream is beginning to seem
more and more like a nightmare, with every passing day.
"Daddy, can you come to my game?"
"Oh, Baby, please don't work late."
Another wasted weekend, and they are slipping away.

'Cause he works all day and lies awake at night.
He tells them things will get better in time.
It'll just take a little more time.

He used to say "Whoever dies with the most toys wins"
But if he loses his soul, what has he gained in the end
I'll take a shack on a rock over a castle in the sand.

Now he works all day and cries alone at night.
It's not getting any better…looks like he's running out of time…

'Cause he worked and he built with his own two hands
and he poured all he had in a castle madewith sand.
But the wind and the rain are coming crashing in.
Time will tell just how long his kingdom stands…
his kingdom stands.

All they ever wanted was you….
All He ever wanted was you…..

You see, Mike had answered a coworker honestly when she'd asked why he always helped out with charity events on weekends. **"I wasn't thinking, so I told the truth. I just said it's what I believed, what my faith taught. Then she asked more questions, and I told her about following Jesus.** That's what did it. Next day, after fifteen years…well, that was it. **My wife told me going to church was one thing, but I'd gone too far and she just couldn't live like that. She left yesterday."**

He hit replay on his laptop, and we listened a minute. "Yea, now I get the torture part. It does feel a bit like I'm dying. But **I know the resurrection's coming, and you know what? I think it's time for a soul-check. I remember Jesus saying something about gaining the world but losing my soul…."**

His face brightened as a sudden realization struck him. "You know, I just realized something. **Jesus has been waiting for me to pick up that cross. My own cross. Because…because….I get it! He's waiting to help me carry it. I get it!"**

And with that, he shut his laptop, gathered his things, said a quick goodbye, and left. I've never seen him again, but I think of him every now and then. How is he? What's he doing now?

Shack on a rock…
Castle in the sand…..

All He wants is….you.
Yep, you…and me.

Carrying our crosses together.
Remember what He said?

*"Come to me, all of you who are weary and carry heavy burdens, and I will give you rest. Take my yoke upon you. Let me teach you, because I am humble and gentle, and you will find rest for your souls. For **my yoke fits perfectly, and the burden I give you is light**." (Matthew 11:28-30, New Living Translation)*

Soul check time!
Got resurrection vision?
Grab your cross, and let's go!!

Reflections

How do we let the possible, imagined consequences of sharing our faith affect us?

What does "pick up your cross and follow Me" mean in your life?

Try, in three sentences or less, to describe what following Jesus means to you. Why are you a Christian?

Jesus admonishes the disciples not to tell anyone in verse 20. Then He challenges them to "pick up crosses" and follow Him, thereby telling the story with their lives. What's the difference between talking and living faith?

7

Blinding Confusion

Six days later Jesus took Peter and the two brothers, James and John, and led them up a high mountain. As the men watched, **Jesus' appearance changed so that his face shone like the sun, and his clothing became dazzling white.**

Suddenly, Moses and Elijah appeared and began talking with Jesus.

Peter blurted out, "Lord, this is wonderful! If you want me to, I'll make three shrines, one for you, one for Moses, and one for Elijah."

But even as he said it, a bright cloud came over them, and a voice from the cloud said, **"This is my beloved Son, and I am fully pleased with him. Listen to him."**

The disciples were terrified and fell face down on the ground.

Jesus came over and touched them. **"Get up," he said, "don't be afraid."** *And when they looked, they saw only Jesus with them. As they descended the mountain, Jesus commanded them, "Don't tell anyone what you have seen until I, the Son of Man, have been raised from the dead."*

His disciples asked, "Why do the teachers of religious law insist that Elijah must return before the Messiah comes?" Jesus replied, **"Elijah is indeed coming first to set everything in order. But I tell you, he has already come, but he wasn't recognized, and he was badly mistreated.** *And soon the Son of Man will also suffer at their hands." Then the* **disciples realized he had been speaking of John the Baptist.**

– Matthew 17: 1-13 (New Living Translation)

Six days later, three of them saw that glory. Jesus took Peter and the brothers, James and John, and led them up a high mountain. **His appearance changed from the inside out, right before their eyes.**

Sunlight poured from his face. His clothes were filled with light. *Then they realized that Moses and Elijah were also there in deep conversation with him.*

Peter broke in, "Master, this is a great moment! What would you think if I built three memorials here on this mountain – one for you, one for Moses, one for Elijah?" While he was going on like this, babbling, a light-radiant cloud enveloped them, and sounding from deep in the cloud a voice: **"This is my son, marked by my love, focus of my delight. Listen to him."**

When the disciples heard it, **they fell flat on their faces, scared to death. But Jesus came over and touched them. "Don't be afraid."** *When they opened their eyes and looked around, all they saw was Jesus, only Jesus.*

Coming down the mountain, Jesus swore them to secrecy. "Don't breathe a word of what you've seen. After the Son of Man is raised from the dead, you are free to talk." The disciples, meanwhile, were asking questions, "Why do the religion scholars say that Elijah has to come first?"

Jesus answered, **"Elijah does come and get everything ready. I'm telling you, Elijah has already come but they** *didn't know him when they saw him. They treated him like dirt, the same way they are about to treat the Son of Man." That's when the disciples realized that all along he had been talking about John the Baptizer.*

- Matthew 17: 1-13 (The Message Version)

* * * * * * * * *

It was the moment they'd all been waiting for. In just a moment, the bandages would come off. **Tuki would know if the surgery had been successful.** After years of pain as the tumor on her optic nerve grew, a gift from a mysterious donor had given her this trip to the United States for the new surgery. With her husband and oldest son at her bedside, the doctor began to remove the bandages from her eyes.

Tuki had tried to visualize what her children would look like from the sound of their voices and what her hands running over their faces had told her over the ten years since she'd gone totally blind. She still remembered the day she'd woken up to total darkness – not even a shadow of light.

Slowly they removed the first layer of bandages. Her husband and son waited, hoping and praying. **Even a little sight would be good,** they'd told each other the night before as they'd prayed together before going to bed. **Even no sight, but no pain either.** Pain medicines (well, any kind of medicine) was almost impossible to get in their small village.

The nurse reached over and dimmed the room lights. Another layer of bandages came off. Tuki's son wondered, *How many layers could there be?*

Finally, the last layer of bandages was removed. All that was left were the eye patches. "Ready?", the doctor asked. "I think so. Yes, I pray so." One patch came off. Tuki's hand flew up to her face, covering her eye. "Aghh! So bright!" Then the other patch came off.

Eyes now tightly shut, hands over her face, Tuki peeked out. With the lights totally dimmed, and shadows dancing around the room, she gradually removed her hands from her face. This was not at all what she thought it would be like. Why, she didn't recognize anyone in the room!

Her husband , tears streaming down his face, called her name, "Tuki! It's me! Can you see me?" She pointed her face in his direction. So bright! But she could make out a face, in fact, several, sort of all blurred together. Tuki's son spoke up. "Let's move back and give Mama a chance. Love you, Mama."

So bright. It seemed like there were two or three of everything. How could this be? She'd only come here to please her family. The village priest had warned her that this blindness, this tumor, was punishment for her grandfather's leaving their village years ago (even before Tuki was born!). She'd believed him – until now.

A small giggle, then a chuckle, then wonderful musical laughter erupted from Tuki as she gasped out, "How could I have been so blind? That missionary that came, he did this. I knew it! He tried to tell me about the God he knew, the One who gave grace freely. It didn't matter what my grandfather did, he told me. Yes, he tried. Oh my. Oh my, my. **Now I truly see. I condemned myself, but Jesus saved me. Yes, He did. What a gift!"**

No, Tuki's physical sight was not perfectly restored. By the time she left the hospital, she could make out faces, and the doctors were hopeful that she'd get better over the following weeks. **Her spiritual sight, however, was returning to 20/20 clarity,** and she couldn't wait to get back to that village priest! Why,God's grace was there all along; she just hadn't noticed it.

* * * * * * * * *

I often catch myself wondering about those disciples. How could they NOT see? Then I look at my own spiritual life and **I realize the many times that I, like they, simply don't see it.** Jesus is right there; grace is staring me in the face – and **I'm blind. Sometimes, like Tuki, Ihave tumors,** things that have grown up in my life to block my grace-vision...and I need them removed. **Good friends andspiritual advisors are true gifts from God,** walking beside me as I undergo this much needed spiritual surgery. Many times we've laughed together as bandages came off and Godly vision was restored.

...and then there are those rare times when God's grace is so perfectly clear it's blinding. It takes me a minute (OK, often more) to adjust my vision to its brightness, and all I can say is, WOW!! Like James and John, **I too want to 'build shelters', containers to hold that grace,** that clear spiritual God-vision. I want to save and savor it. But that's not the Way, the Truth, and the Life.

No, God's grace moves like a never-ending stream, through our lives, passing from one to another. I wonder.... what if that missionary, having discovered the wonder and incredible gift of Jesus Christ....**what if he'd 'built a shelter' and kept it to himself? What if he hadn't shared the Greatest Gift with Tuki?**

The truth is, **God's grace can't be contained.** You can deny it orchoose not to see it. You can, like James and John, try to contain it. Don't you just hear God's sparkling laughter at THAT?!!

The truth is, the more we come to know God, and the more we follow Jesus, God's Son, as our Lord and Savior, the more of God's clear bright grace we'll see, AND..... the more we'll want to let it, like Tuki's laughter, bubble up and out into all we are and all we do!!

Pray, and seek to experience and share more and more of God's clear, bright.....vision!

Reflections

How COULD those disciples not see?

What 'tumors' have grown up in your life that threaten to block your spiritual vision?

Many people speak of Christ as clearing their vision of what God is like. How does knowing Christ help you to see and experience God more clearly?

8

Mountain Movin'

When they arrived at the foot of the mountain, a huge crowd was waiting for them. A man came and knelt before Jesus and said, "Lord, have mercy on my son, because he has seizures and suffers terribly. He often falls into the fire or into the water. So I brought him to your disciples, but they couldn't heal him."

Jesus replied, "You stubborn, faithless people! How long must I be with you until you believe? How long must I put up with you? Bring the boy to me." Then Jesus rebuked the demon in the boy, and it left him. From that moment the boy was well.

Afterward the disciples asked Jesus privately, "Why couldn't we cast out that demon?" "You didn't have enough faith," Jesus told them. **"I assure you, even if you had faith as small as a mustard seed you could say to this mountain, 'Move from here to there,' and it would move. Nothing would be impossible."**

One day after they had returned to Galilee, Jesus told them, "The Son of Man is going to be betrayed. He will be killed, but three days later he will be raised from the dead." And the disciples' hearts were filled with grief.
— Matthew 17: 14-23 (New Revised Standard Version)

Jesus and his disciples returned to the crowd. A man knelt in front of him and said, "Lord, have pity on my son! He has a bad case of epilepsy and often falls into a fire or into water. I brought him to your disciples, but none of them could heal him."

Jesus said, "You people are too stubborn to have any faith! How much longer must I be with you? Why do I have to put up with you? Bring the boy here." Then Jesus spoke sternly to the demon. It went out of the boy, and right then he was healed.

Later the disciples went to Jesus in private and asked him, "Why couldn't we force out the demons?" Jesus replied, "It is because you don't have enough faith! But I can promise you this. **If you had faith no larger than a mustard seed, you could tell this mountain to move from here to there. And it would. Everything would be possible for you."**

While Jesus and his disciples were going from place to place in Galilee, he told them, "The Son of Man will be handed over to people who will kill him. But three days later he will rise to life." All of this made the disciples very sad.
— Matthew 17: 14-23(Contemporary English Version)

* * * * * * * * *

MS – muscular sclerosis. Judy never forgot the day her doctor used those words...to describe her. She remembered thinking, *if I just have enough faith, this will go away. If I just pray the right prayer, pray hard enough – I'll be cured.* But no.

When the expected 'cure' didn't happen, Judy decided she must not have even a kernel - even a tinyseed – offaith left. If she did, God could surely 'move her mountain' of MS. It was that day she gave up. For days (OK, weeks), Judy simply sat. Didn't read. Didn't watch TV. Didn't call friends. Didn't even get out to the yard to mess around in her favorite place – the garden.

No, **Judy just sat by the window, lost in hopelessness.**Spring was happeningright on the other side of that windowpane, but still Judy sat.

Then oneparticularly bad day when her muscles just didn't want to move right (not good to sit in a chair every day, all day), **she noticed something rather odd.** Right in front of her nose, in the cracks of the window ledge, Judy saw threegreen sprouts. In the tiny amount of dirt and debris that had blown into those cracks and stuck there, three tiny seeds had sprouted!

The next day Judy noticed each one had sets of tiny leaves. And she began to rethink her life. The tiny plants, rooted in the hot aluminum window frame, wilted in the hot sun, but perked back up as the shade came, and positively glistened in the morning dew. Good times. Bad times. Wilted times. Fresh, lively times.

Those tiny window-crack flowers became God's good news for Judy. Why, her life was a lot like theirs. Good days. Bad days. Healingbegan for Judy with those flowers. Not 'cure', but soul-deep healing. **Her faith was being healed.** As her faith grew and blossomed, one day she discovered that indeedGod had taken her seed of faith and moved mountains. The MS stayed. Judy's faith grew; her relationship with God and her life as Christ's disciple flourished.

Her MS was a mere hill beside the mountain of her relationship with God. As Judy cultivated and grew those tiny Morning Glory flowers (the ones that had grown in her window crack), she shared them – and their story – with many people. People who had lost hope. People who felt they weren't good enough. People who thought God didn't care about them. The list could go on.......

Yes, from the small seed of her remaining faith, God made a mountain – a mighty Good News peak – out of Judy's life. And boy, did that mountain move!!

* * * * * * * * *

What can God do with our seeds of faith? Why, God can make, and move, mountains!

We plant seeds everywhere we go, in every company we keep.
Maythose seeds be God's, and may we submit our lives as seeds for the spreading of God's Good News in Jesus Christ.

Reflections

What gives you hope when times are bad? Think back to a hard time in your life. What made a "hope-full" difference for you?

Is anyone you know going through tough times right now? How can you be "flowers growing in the cracks" for them?

9

Church Tax

When they reached Capernaum, the collectors of the temple tax came to Peter and said, **"Does your teacher not pay the temple tax?"** *He said, "Yes, he does."*

And when he came home, Jesus spoke of it first, asking, "What do you think, Simon? From whom do kings of the earth take toll or tribute? From their children or from others?"

When Peter said, "From others," Jesus said to him, "Then the children are free."

"However, so that we do not give offense to them, **go to the sea and cast a hook; take the first fish that comes up; and when you open its mouth, you will find a coin; take that and give it to them for you and me."**

- Matthew 17: 24-27 (New Revised Standard Version)

On their arrival in Capernaum, the tax collectors for the Temple tax came to Peter and asked him, **"Doesn't your teacher pay the Temple tax?"** *"Of course he does," Peter replied.*

Then he went into the house to talk to Jesus about it. But before he had a chance to speak, Jesus asked him, "What do you think, Peter? Do kings tax their own people or the foreigners they have conquered?"

"They tax the foreigners," Peter replied. "Well, then," Jesus said, "the citizens are free!

However, we don't want to offend them, so go down to the lake and throw in a line. **Open the mouth of the first fish you catch, and you will find a coin. Take the coin and pay the tax for both of us."**

- Matthew 17: 24-27 (New Living Translation)

* * * * * * * * * *

A rather heated discussion of taxes – sales, income, city, state, you name it, was going on at the next table. All of a sudden, a young voice chipped in with "I don't pay any tax!" A quick answer came back. "Well, it's a good thing the rest of us do. Why, taxes pay for services and things we all need."

The young man thought a minute. **"Well, I wonder then,"** he ventured, "about that ten percent the Bible **talks about.** I mean, don't we all need God? Don't we all need to know about Jesus? And don't we all need church because we're supposed to lean on each other and help each other? Isn't that ten percent supposed to support all that? That's a lot for just ten percent. Don't you guys pay more than that for these taxes you're talking about?

Seems to me what we get from, well, call it 'church tax' if you want, lasts a whole lot longer than anything we get from all those other taxes."

Thus launched a rather interesting discussion of what a "tax" really is. **A woman, obviously exhausted from work, stopped by the table.** "I'll tell you what's taxing", she added to the mix, "work is taxing!" They all looked up at her. "Yeah," she continued, **"ever think that the tax you're talking about isn't just money? What taxes your time?** This young man's got something there. **Ever let God tax your time?**I mean, the government takes it off the top, right? Can't easily get out of the store without paying tax, and just try not paying that April 15ᵗʰ tax – oh yea, right! So how about giving God that ten percent – right off the top – money, time, you name it. **Now THAT time might just grow on you!!**" And with that, she said goodbye and left, a new spring in her step.

Silence fell over the table. Four men sat looking at the door after she left. "Never thought of it that way," one finally said. "Yep, seems like the church does a whole lot more with a whole lot less than the government ever did. I'm reallythinking about that." The young man spoke up again. **"I'm gonna do more than think and talk. I'm gonna DO. I figure God gives 100%; the least I can do is 10%."** And he got up, waved at the other three, and left.

* * * * * * * * * *

Made me think. And think. As it should all of us. **How many of us give God what's left (if there IS anything left!) after we've taken care of everything else?** God gave – and gives – off the top. God gave his most precious Son. **What if God gave us what was left** (if there was anything)? Oh my. You know, in many ways we're just like the 'foreigners' Jesus spoke about. In many ways, a God-centered, Jesus-centered life is foreign to us.

Let's think about this together.When you think of your **'to do' list for the day,** does 'prayer' or 'read Scripture' go at the top? When you plan your vacation, do you say to yourself, "Now I'll have some more time with God!" Or is it more like, "Later, God, later I'll have time for You." But does later REALLY ever come – that often?

How about spending one morning a week in church? Let's see, 4 hours out of perhaps out of 84 (or more) waking hours in your week is **about 4.7% of your time.** Why that leaves another 5.3% for prayer, Bible study, and getting equipped to be the hands and feet of Jesus wherever you go!

And the young man was right, you know. **'Church tax' is SO much more** joy-filled, fulfilling, and MUCH longer lasting!

How about it? I know, it might be a big priority shift, but there are many of us growing into living a 'church tax' life. Won't you join us? How about this week?

Reflections

List the three things you spend the most money on (other than housing):

1.

2.

3.

List the three things you think about the most:

1.

2.

3.

List the three things you spend the most time on/with:

1.

2.

3.

Where would spending time feeding and nurturing your spirit come in – things like spending time with God in prayer and Scripture reading, in church, in Christian service activities, etc. come in?

Think about it either in terms of a percent of your time, thoughts, and money or where it would rank on each of your three lists above.

10

Making the Cut

At about the same time, the disciples came to Jesus asking, **"Who gets the highest rank in God's kingdom?"** *For an answer, Jesus called over a child, whom he stood in the middle of the room, and said, "I'm telling you once and for all, that unless you return to square one and start over like children, you're not even going to get a look at the kingdom, let alone get in.* **Whoever becomes simple and elemental again, like this child, will rank high in God's kingdom.** *What's more, when you receive the childlike on my account, it's the same as receiving me."*

"But if you give them a hard time, bullying or taking advantage of their simple trust, you'll soon wish you hadn't. You'd be better off dropped in the middle of the lake with a millstone around your neck. Doom to the world for giving these God-believing children a hard time! **Hard times are inevitable, but you don't have to make it worse** *– and it's doomsday to you if you do.*

"If your hand or foot gets in the way of God, chop it off *and throw it away. You're better off maimed or lame and alive than the proud owners of two hands and two feet, godless in a furnace of eternal fire. And* **if your eye distracts you from God, pull it out and throw it away.** *You're better off one-eyed and alive than exercising your 20/20 vision from inside the fire of hell."*

- Matthew 18: 1-9 (The Message Version)

At that time the disciples came to Jesus and asked, **"Who is the greatest in the kingdom of heaven?"** *He called a child, whom he put among them, and said, "Truly I tell you, unless you change and become like children, you will never enter the kingdom of heaven.* **Whoever becomes humble like this child is the greatest in the kingdom of heaven.** *Whoever welcomes one such child in my name welcomes me.*

"If any of you put a stumbling block before one of these little ones who believe in me, it would be better for you if a great millstone were fastened around your neck and you were drowned in the depth of the sea.

Woe to the world because of stumbling blocks! **Occasions for stumbling are bound to come,** *but woe to the one by whom the stumbling block comes!*

"If your hand or your foot causes you to stumble, cut it off *and throw it away; it is better for you to enter life maimed or lame than to have two hands or two feet and to be thrown into the eternal fire. And* **if your eye causes you to stumble, tear it out and throw it away;** *it is better for you to enter life with one eye than to have two eyes and to be thrown into the hell of fire."*

- Matthew 18: 1-9 (New Revised Standard Version)

* * * * * * * * *

It was the first week of school, and Ben was excited! Today was his first whole day in first grade, his first time to bring a lunch and eat in the cafeteria! As he unpacked his lunch, he noticed what the kids around him had in theirs. **Dad had packed Ben a turkey sandwich, chips, and a juicy peach. How Ben loved peaches!**

Manuel and Joe, his new lunch friends, had snack boxes, sodas, and candy bars. Boy, those candy bars looked good! But Ben knew his grandma was right when she'd told him, "Benny, honey, candy makes you crazy wild!" Ben didn't need crazy wild right now, not in school. Not on the first day. Not on the second day. Definitely NOT at school, at all.

But Manuel had seen Ben's longing look at his Hershey bar. "Want some?", he asked. Ben thought. And wanted. And thought again. **"Nope," he replied, "I've chopped candy out of my lunch.** Want some of my peach?" Manuel looked at him like he was crazy, smiled, and bit into the Hershey bar.

Joe, on the other hand, thought that peach looked good. "Can I have a bite?" he asked. A minute later, peach juice dripping down his chin, delight in his eyes, he exclaimed, "Wow! Where'd you get these? Can you bring me one tomorrow?"

Well, Ben's aunt and uncle grew them, and that's how a whole table of first graders had peaches for dessert as long as they lasted.

* * * * * * * * *

Interesting what we learn from kids sometimes, isn't it? Ben, Joe, and Manuel were classmates of my youngest son. Dan enjoyed some of the best peaches of his life that fall – all because Ben 'chopped out' candy from his school life.

So how about it?

"Truly I tell you, unless you change and become like children, you will never enter the kingdom of heaven. **Whoever becomes humble like this child is the greatest in the kingdom of heaven.** *Whoever welcomes one such child in my name welcomes me."*

What could we 'chop out' of our lives that makes our life 'crazy wild', that blocks our spiritual growth? Jesus tells us it's better to enter heaven without it than to cling to it and effectively choose hell.

Recently I began thinking about one of my own 'crazy wild' issues. In thinking about how I spend my time, energy, and money, and how I need to lose some weight, I finally connected the dots (I know, some of you are thinking, duh!). I didn't need to buy (and eat) all that food. Chop it off! Take care of the body God created for me. And how about that extra food? Well, we have an emergency food bank at the church. How about that?

I'm working hard to substitute my own 'peach' of exercise for that 'chocolate' of extra food. Ben was on to something big there. And you know what? It's working!

Many of us think of heaven and hell as far away, distant-in-time things. We forget that God has tastes of both right here, right now. Twenty-five pounds ago, I could have told you about more fatigue, tired knees and back, and more 'hellish' things. Now I can share with you a few great 'heavenly' things: moreenergy, a better attitude, and a bounce in my step.

Chop, chop! It's a growth process, you know. Closer and closer to a life paying attention to the best God created us to be. Closer and closer to treating ourselves like what we are created to be – images of God!

No, **making 'the cut' isn't always easy, but the results are so good!** Startsmall. What can you 'make the cut' with? Chop, chop!
Maybe you'll score some 'peachy' rewards too!

Reflections

What comes to mind when you think of the words "be like a child"? Is it attractive to you? Why or why not?

How can you notice and welcome "the child" in others?

Where (and what) are the "Hershey bars" in your life? The "peaches"?

11

Ninety-Nine Percent

"Don't be cruel to any of these little ones! I promise you that their angels are always with my Father in heaven. Let me ask you this. What would you do if you had a hundred sheep and one of them wandered off? **Wouldn't you leave the ninety-nine on the hillside and go look for the onethat had wandered away?***

"I am sure that finding it would make you happier than having the ninety-nine that never wandered off. **That's how it is with your Father in heaven. He doesn't want any of these little ones to be lost."**

– *Matthew 18: 10-14 (Contemporary English Version)*

"Beware that you don't despise a single one of these little ones. For I tell you that in heaven their angels are always in the presence of my heavenly Father.

"If a shepherd has one hundred sheep, and one wanders away and is lost, what will he do? **Won't he leave the ninety-nine others and go out into the hills to search for the lost one?** *And if he finds it, he will surely rejoice over it more than over the ninety-nine that didn't wander away!*

In the same way, **it is not my heavenly Father's will that even one of these little ones should perish.**

– *Matthew 18: 10-14 (New Living Translation)*

* * * * * * * * * *

"100 cute little sheep on the hill,
100 cute little sheep.
One wanders off, oh, no, it's lost!
99 cute little sheep on the hill,
99 cute little sheep on the hill,...."

So began the new song a little girl shared with the congregation one Sunday morning during children's sharing time.

Ever feel parts of your life 'wander off'? I have.
Pretty soon, another of your 'sheep' has wandered off. And another.
One small part at a time, your life moves away from the Shepherd.
Before you know it, you're singing the 90th (or perhaps 50th) verse of that little girl's song.

One tiny bit at a time, you begin to ignore Jesus Christ. Oh, He's still hunting for your 'lost sheep', all right. But you've stopped noticing. But here's the thing.

He never gives up. Ever.

Even if you ever lose all your 'sheep', and you've lost sight of the Shepherd, He's never lost sight of you. He's as close as your next breath.

Go back and read that Scripture again. Go ahead, you've got time.....

"...it is not my heavenly Father's will that even one of these little ones should perish."

That's right, **it's not God's will that any part of your life would be separated from him.** Not even one one-hundredth of it. Jesus, your Shepherd, is out searching for those parts of you that are lost. **Accept His help.** Claim (or reclaim) Him as the Shepherd of your life.

Yes, God and heaven rejoice when those 'lost' parts of our lives are found.

Can't you just see the Shepherd's face now?

Reflections

How are churches you know of following Jesus' example of 'seeking the one sheep'? How do they do this effectively and genuinely (or do they)?

If you are involved in a church, how does it feel to be one of the "ninety-nine sheep"?

What keeps churches more interested in the "ninety-nine sheep" than the "one sheep" whom Jesus focuses on in this Scripture?

12

True Community

"If another member of the church sins against you, go and point out the fault when the two of you are alone. If the member listens to you, you have regained that one.

But if you are not listened to, take one or two others along with you, so that every word may be confirmed by the evidence of two or three witnesses.

If the member refuses to listen to them, tell it to the church; and if the offender refuses to listen even to the church, let such a one be to you as a Gentile and a tax collector.

Truly I tell you, whatever you bind on earth will be bound in heaven, and whatever you loose on earth will be loosed in heaven.

Again, truly I tell you, if two of you agree on earth about anything you ask, it will be done for you by my Father in heaven.

For where two or three are gathered in my name, I am there among them."

- Matthew 18: 15-20 (New Revised Standard Version)

"If another believer sins against you, go privately and point out the fault. If the other person listens and confesses it, you have won that person back.

But if you are unsuccessful, take one or two others with you and go back again, so that everything you say may be confirmed by two or three witnesses. If that person still refuses to listen, take your case to the church. If the church decides you are right, but the other person won't accept it, treat that person as a pagan or a corrupt tax collector.

I tell you this: Whatever you prohibit on earth is prohibited in heaven, and whatever you allow on earth is allowed in heaven.

"I also tell you this: If two of you agree down here on earth concerning anything you ask, my Father in heaven will do it for you.

For where two or three gather together because they are mine, I am there among them."

- Matthew 18: 15-20 (New Living Translation)

* * * * * * * * * *

She wandered in one Sunday. It was the Sunday that Mary, one of our church 'kitchen angels', came early and baked cookies. The smell wafting from the kitchen was, well, words can't even describe the delicious anticipation.

"Smells real good in here. Whatcha cooking?" Mary looked up to see an interesting sight. Fashionably

34

'ripped' jeans (in some interesting places, I might add) topped by a **Wiccan 'goddess rules' t-shirt greeted her eyes.**

That didn't stop Mary. Nope. Soon, Nirvana (yep, that's what she called herself) was settled in the kitchen stirring batter and putting cookies on platters for the after-worship fellowship later that morning.

"So what do you do here?" This was the question Nirvana asked that first morning which would come back again and again, because Mary never forgot that 'Holy Spirit morning' in the church kitchen.

So Nirvana came to church. Really. It was a new and interesting experience. You might even call it an adventure – not just for her, but for all of us. She was seeking, looking for, as she called it, the 'missing link' between her and God. Soon Nirvana opened up and began bringing her honest questions to the adult Bible study/ discussion group.

"So, what do you all do to celebrate the winter solstice?", she asked one Sunday morning. "Is it in here?" She flipped to the table of contents in her new Bible. "I got one of these this week; it's very interesting!" Silence. More silence. I mean, what do you say to that? All eyes went to the class leader.

"Well, I think....I think that's sort of a pagan thing. I don't know that much about it...."
"I do. Let me tell you about it. It's a way of, well sort of connecting with the goddess, um, I mean God, yeah..." So it was that the adult class learned about Wiccan solstice observance.

The storm came after class –in the pastor**'s study.** Several people, including the class leader, came for advice. **"What do we do with THIS?"** was pretty much the universal appeal. "Have you talked with her about how you feel?", the pastor asked them. The answer came quickly. "Well, **she's wrong, that's all. I tried to tell her** we don't believe in all that stuff. Told her that folks who did, well, we all know where they're headed..."

"Yeah, and we're doing just what the Bible said to do." Bill whipped out his Bible and flipped right to, you guessed it, this week's Scripture passage. "Yep, yep,...", he said as he checked off the verses. "Well, I guess it's time for us to get a group together and visit her, and if that doesn't work, well, she'll just have to go back to those pagan witch friends of hers."

Just then Mary spoke up. "Give me that Good Book, Bill." He handed it over. "Mmmm hmm.....mmmm hmmmm....just like I thought."

Mary, finished reviewing the text, looked up at them. "I've got just one question for you. How did (and would) Jesus treat unbelievers and tax collectors? Seems to me He kept inviting them. Seems to me He met them right where they were. Why I remember after my Fred passed and I was all wrong in my spirit, seems to me y'all welcomed me too, met me right where I was too – even when I doubted God completely. **Did you know it took 'bout everything I had just to walk in these church doors? Can you even guess how much it took Nirvana to walk in here?"**

Silence.

"But she....she..." One of the women began.
"Makes you uncomfortable, doesn't she? Yep, me too. But it didn't stop Jesus, and it isn't stopping me either. **This church isn't just any community.** Nope, it's Jesus Christ's community. I don't know about you, but that's Who I'm true to. Now, Nirvana and I, we're going out to that new restaurant over on Red Bridge. **I'm betting Jesus**

is walking right next to her, and I want to be there when she sees Him. How about you?" With that, a smiling Mary left.

That changed everything. The Sunday adult Bible study/discussion group began to meet Nirvana where she was, helping her see the Jesus in her life, helping her claim the transforming power of the Holy Spirit, and how exciting it was! Why, God was creating a new Nirvana right in their midst! You should have seen the celebration they put on six months later when Nirvana was baptized into the Body of Christ – not a dry eye in that class.

* * * * * * * * * *

So how about it? **Most of us read the 'rules' of this Scripture passage as a set of directions.** You know, do 'a' then 'b' then 'c', and if that doesn't work, well, give it up! Wasn't it a wonderful, Spirit-filled thing that the day Nirvana first walked into the church kitchen Mary was there? Mary and Nirvana, **'two gathered together', with Jesus in their midst. Mary knew Jesus; Nirvana didn't.** Through Mary the 'kitchen angel', Jesus welcomed Nirvana, just as she was. Through Mary, and the true community in that church, God grew Nirvana – loving her, accepting her, gently leading her from where she was to a whole new life – an eternal life of freedom in Jesus Christ.

How's our "true community" score? Is our welcome 'in the name of Christ' one that He would own? **Jesus really does meet us right where we are, but refuses to leave us there.** He "walks with us, and talks with us – along life's narrow way", as the old song, "He Lives", says. Can we do any less with and for our brothers and sisters? (not just in our churches, but also in our neighborhoods, at work, at school, ...)

"Love your neighbor as yourself" – Jesus quotes this as one of the two bedrock commandments (Matthew 22:39). How about it?

Reflections

Who do you identify with more in this story: Mary, Nirvana, or the class leader? Why do you think this is?

What is "true community" to you?

In what ways do you experience Jesus walking beside you "along life's narrow way"?

13

Enough is Enough....?

*At that point Peter got up the nerve to ask, **"Master, how many times do I forgive a brother or sister who hurts me? Seven?"***

Jesus replied, "Seven! Hardly. Try seventy times seven.

"The kingdom of God is like a king who decided to square accounts with his servants. As he got underway, one servant was brought before him who had run up a debt of a hundred thousand dollars. He couldn't pay up, so the king ordered the man, along with his wife, children, and goods, to be auctioned off at the slave market.

*"The poor wretch **threw himself at the king's feet and begged, 'Give me a chance and I'll pay it all back.' Touched by his plea, the king let him off, erasing the debt.***

"The servant was no sooner out of the room when he came upon one of his fellow servants who owed him ten dollars. He seized him by the throat and demanded, 'Pay up!Now!'

"The poor wretch threw himself down and begged, 'Give me a chance and I'll pay it all back.' But he wouldn't do it. He had him arrested and put in jail until the debt was paid. When the other servants saw this going on, they were outraged and brought a detailed report to the king.

*"The king summoned the man and said, **'You evil servant! I forgave your entire debt when you begged me for mercy. Shouldn't you be compelled to be merciful to your fellow servant who asked you for mercy?'** The king was furious and put the screws to the man until he paid back his entire debt. And that's exactly what my father in heaven is going to do to each one of you who doesn't forgive unconditionally anyone who asks for mercy."*

- Matthew 18: 21-35 (The Message Version)

* * * * * * * * *

"Enough is Enough!!"

The loud, exasperated parent's voice carried long and far through the localKmart.
Just in case we didn't quite catch it the first time, mere seconds later came the follow-up:

"I said NO! ENOUGH IS ENOUGH!!"

* * * * * * * * *

Now consider this thought-provoking comment, made by a young girl at Communion. Picture a cute-as-a-button girl with beautiful braids reaching up to take a piece of the Communion loaf.....a BIG piece. Her mom whispers, "No, honey. That's too much;**just take a SMALL piece – that's enough**." Her answer carries back several rows:

"But Mom, I didn't think you could ever get enough Jesus!"

* * * * * * * * * *

The disciples are more in the first scene, in the parent'sframe of mind. How much IS enough?

Jesus, however, is more in the little girls' frame of mind. Call it a 'God frame of mind'. How many times is God willing to forgive? More than I can think of! Jesus Himself is the demonstration of that. Forgiveness is allowing another (or one's self) to be human, imperfect, and fallible.

Isn't it interesting that (OK, be honest now) **many times we really resemble the forgiven servant who turned around and refused forgiveness to others.** It's just not that easy to forgive, is it? Many times we confuse forgiveness (allowing that we are all human) with forget-ness (refusing to learn from our experiences). Perhaps better than the commonly expressed, "forgive and forget", the instruction for human beings should more accurately be, "forgive and learn".

Well, the truth is that we'll never have the forgiveness capacity of God (and thank goodness we're NOT God!), but **we are called to get better and better at forgiveness as disciples of Christ.** Better and better..........hmmm.

So, as the disciples ask, **is that seven times? That's tough enough**, but Jesus answers with a much higher benchmark – 70 X 7!!

Jesus calls us to a life of persistent, growing maturity in our faith – a faith lived out every day in all the situations and relationships of our lives.

So just how do we get from where we are (most of us are far more like the parent in the local Kmart than the little girl at Communion) **to where Jesus is calling us?**

We intentionally build our connection with God as disciples of Jesus.
We study the Bible – on our own, just us and God – and with others (for example, Bible study and discussion groups).
We spend time in regular prayer.
We get away for intentional time growing and enriching our faith.

So wherever you are, whether it's trying to forgive for the first time, the seventh time, or (bless you) somewhere between that and 490th (70 X 7th) time, **study, prayer, and intentional retreat time spent on your faith journey are precious – and necessary.** It's a matter of priorities. Eternal ones.

Take the time. Make the time.
Keep trying.....7 times.....70 X 7 times....whatever it takes.

God will never, ever give up on you.
God will never, ever have 'enough' of you. Ever. Even far beyond 70 X 7!!

Reflections

What does the difference between forgiving (allowing ourselves and others to be human) and forgetting (refusing to learn from experiences) look like in your life?

How are the ability to forgive and an active and growing faith life related?

Why do people give up trying to grow and enrich their faith lives?

What would you say to someone who's given up?

14

The "D" Word

After Jesus had finished saying these things, he left Galilee and went southward to the region of Judea and into the area east of the Jordan River. Vast crowds followed him there, and he healed their sick.

Some Pharisees came and tried to trap him with this question: **"Should a man be allowed to divorce his wife for any reason?"**

"Haven't you read the Scriptures?" Jesus replied. "They record that from the beginning 'God made them male and female.'" And he said, "This explains why a man leaves his father and mother and is joined to his wife, and the two are united into one. Since they are no longer two but one, **let no one separate them, for God has joined them together."**

"Then why did Moses say a man could merely write an official letter of divorce and send her away?" they asked.

Jesus replied, "Moses permitted divorce as a concession to your hard-hearted wickedness, but it was not what God had originally intended. And I tell you this, a man who divorces his wife and marries another commits adultery – unless his wife has been unfaithful. "

- Matthew 19: 1-9 (New Living Translation)

When Jesus finished teaching, he left Galilee and went to the part of Judea that is east of the Jordan River. Large crowds followed him, and he healed their sick people.

Some Pharisees wanted to test Jesus. They came up to him and asked, "Is it right for a man to divorce his wife for just any reason?"

Jesus answered, "Don't you know that in the beginning the Creator made a man and a woman? That's why a man leaves his father and mother and gets married. He becomes like one person with his wife. Then they are no longer two people, but one. And **no one should separate a couple that God has joined together."**

The Pharisees asked Jesus, "Why did Moses say that a man could write out divorce papers and send his wife away?"

Jesus replied, "You are so heartless! That's why Moses allowed you to divorce your wife. But from the beginning God did not intend it to be that way. I say that if your wife has not committed some terrible sexual sin, you must not divorce her to marry someone else. If you do, you are unfaithful."

- Matthew 19: 1-9 (Contemporary English Version)

* * * * * * * * *

So **who's the 'no one' this Scripture refers to** in saying that,"...*no one should separate a couple that God has joined together.*"?

Oh, perhaps you mean maybe **Jesus is talking to more than just the wife and husband?** Well.....yes indeed!

Consider these two conversation 'snippets' overheard this past week:

"Oh, girlfriend, **if only she knew what Julie did last year.** If she just knew, she wouldn't be talking to her, let alone hanging with her. Somebody's got to tell her!"
"Yeah, it's like they're best friends now or something. **We've got to break THAT up for sure!**"

and this...
"They're brothers, did you know that?"
"I know, but **Bill's said some rotten things about John. We should warn John...**"
His friend grimaced. "Well, maybe..."
"Maybe? MAYBE?" An incredulous expression sprang up on the first man's face.
"Yea, **but they are brothers, you know. Brothers.** We've known them since high school. Maybe we could talk to both of them..."
I could tell the friend was beginning to think as he answered, "How about if you call Bill and I'll call John. Let's pray about it."
And the two men bowed their heads and did just that.

* * * * * * * * * *

Sometimes it's easy to narrow the focus and application of what Jesus says....until it really doesn't apply to us (or perhaps applies, but in a limited, safe way). Is Jesus only talking of married couples here?

It's true thatHis main focus is on wives and husbands. But as the 'others' in this scenario, **doesn't it apply to others 'whom God has joined together'?** Brothers? Sisters? Best friends? I'm sure you can think of others as well. God brings others into our lives, many times 'joining' our lives together for varying lengths of time. How do we honor that in our own lives? In the lives of those around us?

How do we respond when those we know are wounded by someone in close relationship with them? Do we pray and act to be instruments of peace, healing, and reconciliation? Or do our words and actions damage (or even destroy) relationships?

Let's pray to do our best to be reconcilers, healers, and peacemakers, walking in Jesus' footsteps as his disciples.

Reflections

How do we honor those in our own lives whom God has "brought us together" with?

How <u>do</u> we respond when those we know are wounded by someone in a close relationship? How could we improve that response?

15

Single and Seeking...What?

His disciples said to him, "If such is the case of a man with his wife, it is better not to marry."
*But he said to them, **"Not everyone can accept this teaching, but only those to whom it is given.***
"For there are eunuchs who have been so from birth, and there are eunuchs who have been made eunuchs by others, and there are eunuchs who have made themselves eunuchs for the sake of the kingdom of heaven. Let anyone accept this who can."
- Matthew 19: 10-12 (New Revised Standard Version)

The disciples said, "If that's how it is between a man and a woman, it's better not to get married."
*Jesus told them "Only those **people who have been given the gift of staying single** can accept this teaching.*
*Some people are unable to marry because of birth defects or because of what someone has done to their bodies. **Others stay single in order to serve God better.** Anyone who can accept this teaching should do so."*
- Matthew 19: 10-12 (Contemporary English Version)

* * * * * * * * *

The two kids settled in at the table while their moms waited in line to place their order at the local Starbucks. They were obviously continuing a conversation begun before their arrival....
"Well, I'm **never** getting **married**!"
"**I'm** getting married and **having ten kids!**"

Now THAT really got my attention. **Has this boy really thought about that?** TEN kids? Wow. These **boys looked to be around 8 or 9 years old**. Just kids. But glancing at their intent faces,
I could tell they were serious.

Their moms had moved to the counter to pick up the drinks by now, but the boys' conversation continued.

"Well, **my uncle's not married, and he's happy.** He does all kinds of stuff, like next year he's **taking me with him on a mission trip**...all the way to Washington! **Just try to do THAT with your ten kids!**"

"**Well, I figure with ten kids, I'll have my OWN mission team!**"

About then the moms got to the table with the drinks and the conversation shifted to other things, but **these boys had made me think** (and laugh a bit) about the many and varied ways God gifts and calls us.

It's easy to look at negative and/or positive examples of married or single life around us and make our own life decisions based on that. Many times it's much easier than genuinely seeking the life God is equipping and calling us to.

Sometimes God calls usuniquely in the different seasons of our lives. Some have married 'seasons' and single 'seasons'. Others have lifetimes of ministry as singles, still others as married persons.

It's important to remember that God seeks to work in us and through us in all the varied times of our lives.

Are you single? Married? **How is God using your life right now?**

Your life right now, whether single or married, is full of God's gifts and ministry calling! Are you letting God work in and through your life, transforming you and those around you, deepening and enriching your faith as you walk ever closer through life as Christ's disciple?

Hear the words of Luke 11:9-10:
"And so I tell you, **keep on asking**, and you will be given what you ask for. **Keep on looking**, and you will find. **Keep on knocking**, and the door will be opened.

For **everyone who asks, receives. Everyone who seeks, finds. And the door is opened to everyone who knocks."** (New Living Translation)

In all this, too, remember that what we think we're asking for isn't always what we're really asking for. God knows our gifts. God knows what we truly need. And **God is with us always as we ask, seek, and knock. In singleness. In married life. Always.**

Reflections

How would you describe a full, purposeful single life?

How about a full, purposeful married life?

How can we let our married or single life situation interfere with – or strengthen – God's gifting and call on us?

16

Seen... and Heard

*Then little children were being brought to him in order that he might lay his hands on them and pray. The disciples spoke sternly to those who brought them;but Jesus said, **"Let the little children come to me, and do not stop them; for it is to such as these that the kingdom of heaven belongs."***
And he laid his hands on them and went on his way.

- Matthew 19: 13-15 (New Revised Standard Version)

*Some children were brought to Jesus so he could lay his hands on them and pray for them. The disciples told them not to bother him. But Jesus said, **"Let the children come to me. Don't stop them! For the Kingdom of Heaven belongs to such as these."***
And he put his hands on their heads and blessed them before he left.

- Matthew 19: 13-15 (New Living Translation)

* * * * * * * * *

Into the relative silenceof waiting for the Sunday morning worship to begin came a wonderful (or awful), charming (or awful), joyful (or awful).......**procession of 20-30 children, all singing this hymn –loud and clear:**

"When we all get to heaven, what a day of rejoicing that will be... when we all see Jesus, we'll sing and shout the victory!!" (Eliza Hewitt & Emily Wilson, 1898)
Picture these kids parading in with maracas, tambourines, clappers, etc...... smiles on their faces, with joyful worship just pouring from them!

Now picture the faces of the folks in the congregation. Some wonderful (or awful), some utterly charmed (or awful), some joyful (or awful)...you get it, I'm sure.

Feedback after the service was much the same. **Some loved it** – said it was the high spiritual point of their week. **And then...there were others.** The 'seen and not heard' crowd. Hmmm....

I wonder what would happen if we were as excited about Jesus as we are about, say, our favorite sports team? **What if** we got as excited about Jesus, (the eternal Good News) as we do about the new restaurant with the fabulous food, or the new movie, or......

Think about it. Think about the last time you were so excited about something like that, you just had to tell someone. Kids are like that. When they get excited about something, they just have to tell everyone around!

So what happens that makes us think that it's OK to share our favorite sports team, restaurant, recipe, movie, whatever......but not our new and transforming life as disciples of Christ?

Dare I say it? OK, here it is: **What makes us so much more excited about these temporary things** (yes, they're all good and exciting, but...) than we are about Jesus and God's eternal saving grace?

Could it be that we just take God's grace for granted? Do we take Jesus for granted?

The children who came to Jesus that day did not take Him for granted – they were SO EXCITED! God's Son, the Messiah, was right there – right in front of them! Wow! They came running, and Jesus was waiting, arms outstretched to them, welcoming them - **despite the disciples 'proper' expectations of 'seen and not heard' children.**

The children coming into church that day joyfully singing didn't take Jesus for granted either. Their voices, their clapping, their joyful parade said it all. They knew Jesus was right there, with them, right then...... **despite the 'proper' expectations of some folks that they be 'seen and not heard'.**

How about us? **Is Jesus to be 'seen and not heard' in our lives?**

Hear again the words of Jesus: *"Let the children come to me. Don't stop them! <u>For the Kingdom of Heaven belongs to such as these</u>."*
So how will we, in our own style and with our own gifts, 'sing and shout the victory'?
How will we be like the children Jesus shows us as examples of living grace? They were certainly NOT in the 'seen and not heard' crowd.

Oh, no, **the children of God's kingdom of Good News are definitely SEEN and HEARD!!**

Reflections

What was the last thing you were so excited about that you just HAD to tell someone?

Why are people less likely to share the Good News of Christ than they are to share other, much more temporary things?

Name some ways in which (other than overt "Do you know Jesus?") Christians – maybe even you! – can share the difference following Jesus makes in their lives.

17

REALLY Rich

Someone came to Jesus with this question: "Teacher, what good things must I do to have eternal life?" *"Why ask me about what is good?" Jesus replied. "Only God is good. But to answer your question, you can receive eternal life if you keep the commandments."*

"Which ones?" the man asked. And Jesus replied: " 'Do not murder. Do not commit adultery. Do not steal. Do not testify falsely.

Honor your father and mother. Love your neighbor as yourself.' "

"I've obeyed all these commandments," the young man replied. "What else must I do?"

*Jesus told him, "If you want to be perfect, **go and sell all you have and give the money to the poor, and you will have treasure in heaven.** Then come, follow me."*

*But when the young man heard this, **he went sadly away because he had many possessions.***

Then Jesus said to his disciples, "I tell you the truth, it is very hard for a rich person to get into the Kingdom of Heaven. I say it again—it is easier for a camel to go through the eye of a needle than for a rich person to enter the Kingdom of God!"

- Matthew 19: 16-24 (New Living Translation)

Another day, a man stopped Jesus and asked, "Teacher, what good thing must I do to get eternal life?" *Jesus said, "Why do you question me about what's good? GOD is the One who is good. **If you want to enter the life of God, just do what he tells you."***

The man asked, "What in particular?"

Jesus said, "Don't murder, don't commit adultery, don't steal, don't lie, honor your father and mother, and love your neighbor as you do yourself."

The young man said, "I've done all that. What's left?"

***"If you want to give it all you've got," Jesus replied, "go sell your possessions; give everything to the poor. All your wealth will then be in heaven.** Then come follow me."*

***That was the last thing the young man expected to hear.** And so, crestfallen, he walked away. **He was holding on tight to a lot of things**, and he couldn't bear to let go.*

As he watched him go, Jesus told his disciples, "Do you have any idea how difficult it is for the rich to enter God's kingdom? Let me tell you, it's easier to gallop a camel through a needle's eye than for a rich man to enter God's kingdom."

- Matthew 19: 16-24 (The Message Version)

* * * * * * * * * *

The line of folks filed past the pastor and greeters as they left the worship service one Sunday. Among the comments shared with hugs and handshakes came this question from a first time guest: **"So how do YOU say I can get rich? My old church lied about that every Sunday!"**

You see, **this man had just declared bankruptcy, due in large part to his striving to follow the financial stewardship program his 'old' church assigned him.** This church required its members (and regular participants) to disclose their annual income, sign pledge contracts for 10%, and then billed them monthly. Even when he lost his job, his wife was diagnosed with cancer, and a severe storm damaged his home, the church leadership required him to pay. They called. They visited. And **they sent his pledge contract to a collection agency**. All this while each Sunday he heard about how those who paid cheerfully got more money from God in return. **To get rich, he had to pay God (his words).**

We call this a 'prosperity gospel'. The 'prayer of Jabez' (1 Chronicles 4:9-10) is one Scripture that is often quoted. Interestingly enough, these two little verses are surrounded by proof of real and complete blessing – family, kinship, and community. Real riches. True riches.

"So what brought you to church this morning?" I asked him. OK, maybe not the best question, but with God's help it worked out well. In his place, I don't know if I would have set foot in another church - ever again!

As he told his story, **he ended by sharing that he had actually been planning to see a movie.** As he drove the 20 miles or so into town, he was **searching for a radio station. He found a 'real preacher'** talking about what it meant to be TRULY rich. The man was discussing the Scripture from Matthew's Gospel which is printed above.

"What that guy on the radio said, **it was God, touching me like He hasn't touched me in a long time," he began. "It was like it spoke right to me!** It's easy, the preacher said, to think it's only about money, **easy to think it's ALL about money.** Then he asked us, 'Where's your REAL treasure? Is it heavenly treasure? Are you thinking, praying, and working with God in your WHOLE life? Because if you are, **having no money doesn't make you broke. No, stepping away from God is what makes you broke.'"**

"Then you know what that radio preacher said next? He said, **'If you're listening to me right now because somebody told you God only wants your money, get to a REAL church – right now.** Get your main focus off those worldly things and onto heavenly things.'"

"So you know what? Just then **I happened to be driving right past your church.** So I came in. You're different. Nobody asked for my income; nobody gave me a bill; nobody preached about the payback God was going to give me if I, **well.....I just have one question."**

"Is this a REAL church? Will you help me learn to be REALLY rich?"

It's much easier to focus on one thing; much easier to align our focus on what the world values (money, material possessions).

Real life is so much more. And God is a real God, loving us and growing us in our real lives, guiding and transforming us to live real lives that are wonderfully, incredibly,...

REALLY rich!

Reflections

Name five things that could be considered "treasures"? What makes each of them a "treasure"?

Describe a "real" church? What would it feel like? What would the people be like? The leaders? What kinds of things would this church be doing?

Many people "get their church" on the radio, television, and/or online. How "'real" is this kind of church? Why might people who are able to physically go to a church prefer to "get their church" this way?

18

The End of the Line

When the disciples heard this, they were greatly astounded and said, "Then who can be saved?"
But Jesus looked at them and said, "For mortals it is impossible, but for God all things are possible."
Then Peter said in reply, "Look, we have left everything and followed you. What then will we have?"
*Jesus said to them, "Truly I tell you, at the renewal of all things, when the Son of Man is seated on the throne of his glory, you who have followed me will also sit on twelve thrones, judging the twelve tribes of Israel. And everyone who has left houses or brothers or sisters or father or mother or children or fields, for my name's sake, will receive a hundredfold, and will inherit eternal life. But **many who are first will be last, and the last will be first.***

- Matthew 19: 25-30 (New Revised Standard Version)

The disciples were staggered. "Then who has any chance at all?"
Jesus looked hard at them and said, "No chance at all if you think you can pull it off yourself. Every chance in the world if you trust God to do it."
Then Peter chimed in. "We left everything and followed you. What do we get out of it?"
*Jesus replied, "Yes, you have followed me. In the re-creation of the world, when the Son of Man will rule gloriously, you who have followed me will also rule, starting with the twelve tribes of Israel. And not only you, but anyone who sacrifices home, family, fields – whatever – because of me will get it all back a hundred times over, not to mention the considerable bonus of eternal life. **This is the Great Reversal: many of the first ending up last, and the last first."***

- Matthew 19: 25-30 (The Message Version)

* * * * * * * * * *

As the long line of little ducks made their way across the water behind their mom, I almost missed it. But then I noticed something interesting. Every now and then, the last little duck (the smallest of them all) would turn around, dart back a bit, and grab something with its little beak. Then it would paddle frantically to catch back up with the line.

I had gone out to the little pond to pray for a friend. **Staci had just failed the professional counseling board exam – for the second time.** "What does God WANT?" had been her anguished cry on the phone a short time earlier.

I had seen Staci in action. She was an excellent counselor. Her life had been absolutely crazy. In the last year, both her parents had died and two of her siblings had been diagnosed with cancer. She was also extremely competitive, having spent years as a competitive long distance runner. **All she knew was that she HAD to pass that exam,** because she had a job waiting for her (better than the local fast food place where she was working then). Staci also suffered from debilitating migraine headaches, which were usually triggered by stress. Oh, and did I mention test anxiety? She'd been in treatment for that for years.

"I'm starting at the back of the line, in the back of the pack. What am I going to DO?" This was the question that kept coming up as she prepared for the board exam.

As I watched the line of little ducklings, **that littlest one at the back of the line darted back again.** I began to watch, trying to figure out why. Then I saw it – a flying piece of what looked like bread! And the little duck wheeled around, darted back, snapped it up, and began the frantic journey to catch up again.

Only **this time was different.** A couple of the other little ducklings had noticed. Almost with one movement, the whole line turned around! Now it was the small duckling they were all following! The little boy who was throwing bread jumped up and down excitedly as all the little ducklings and the mom duck zipped back to follow. Now the littlest duckling, who had been struggling so hard to catch up, was indeed the star of the show! I watched as the boy threw bread out onto the water until his whole bag was gone. His smile was radiant – these ducks had made his day.

And **so I began to pray for Staci,** who felt like that littlest duckling – at the back of the line, destined to never 'catch up', to pass her exam like all her friends had already done.

A few months went by. One day I got an excited call from her. "Guess what?" she began, "I've met a few other people just like me! We've figured it out – we're not as stupid as we thought!" (I could have told her that – she had an almost a 4.0 grade point average). She shared with me that she'd decided to pray for ALL those who, like her, hadn't passed the boards. **God began sending her little encouragements.** She met a colleague in the local coffee shop who hadn't passed either (his third try). Then she met another at the library. Then the counseling practice who'd offered her the job (when she passed the board exam) called to ask if she'd be interested in helping lead a therapy group for people struggling with career adversity. Yes, they knew she hadn't passed yet, but **'something' told them Staci was just the person they needed.**

Staci was transformed from the littlest, smallest-feeling duckling at the back of the line to one who led others to new lives and new ministries. Staci and her two new friends founded a new career counseling and coaching practice (after all three passed their boards – on the next try) which has helped and ministered to many people.

Where in your life are you feeling like that littlest duckling?
God can use that, you know. Just like Staci.
Pray about that. **Stay open to God's leading.**

It's not 'the end of the line'. It's only the beginning! We serve and worship a God of awesome new beginnings!

So what do we 'get out of it'? Oh yes, we often think like that, just like Jesus' disciples. Well, listen again: *"This is the Great Reversal: many of the first ending up last, and the last first."*

May you be open to the wonderful things God can accomplish in and through you in the midst of your 'end of the line' experiences and times.

Reflections

How can we stay open to God's leading and strengthening us when we find ourselves in positions like Staci and that little duck in the back of the line?

How can you encourage others who find themselves in challenging situations when they feel like just giving up?

19

It's Not Fair!

"For the Kingdom of Heaven is like the owner of an estate who went out early one morning to hire workers for his vineyard. He agreed to pay the normal daily wage and sent them out to work.

"At nine o'clock in the morning he was passing through the marketplace and saw some people standing around doing nothing. So he hired them, telling them he would pay them whatever was right at the end of the day.

"At noon and again around three o'clock he did the same thing.

"At five o'clock that evening he was in town again and saw some more people standing around. He asked them, 'Why haven't you been working today?' They replied, 'Because no one hired us.' The owner of the estate told them, 'Then go on out and join the others in my vineyard.'

*"That evening he told the foreman to call the workers in and pay them, beginning with the last workers first. **When those hired at five o'clock were paid, each received a full day's wage.***

*"**When those hired earlier came to get their pay, they assumed they would receive more.** But they, too, were paid a day's wage. When they received their pay, **they protested,** 'Those people worked only one hour, and yet you've paid them just as much as you paid us who worked all day in the scorching heat.'*

*"He answered one of them, '**Friend, I haven't been unfair!** Didn't you agree to work all day for the usual wage? Take it and go. I wanted to pay this last worker the same as you. Is it against the law for me to do what I want with my money? **Should you be angry because I am kind?'***

"And so it is, that many who are first now will be last then; and those who are last now will be first then."

- Matthew 20: 1-16 (New Living Translation)

* * * * * * * * * *

"I don't know ifwe can afford this."

The couple's eyes brimmed with tears.

The wife spoke first. "You know, we don't have much money, and Mom's medical care has used up what little we had to help. **All she's got is her social security."**

"This place is so nice.Really. But..." Tears welled up and spilled out the corners of his eyes as he looked over at his wife. "I think Mom would like this too. Maybe you know a place like this that we could afford....?"

Two pairs of hopeful eyes looked at the assisted living community administrator.

"Well", he said, "Let me make a call. I'll be right back."

He was smiling as he returned. **"I think we can help you. You see, a while back a man named Sam lived here.** He died here too, in fact. He met lots of people just like you, coming in to check the place out. Sam loved to talk to them. Why he'd even give them tours! Paid his whole way, Sam did, and we never knew until he died,... well, the truth is that Sam was a multi-millionaire. He couldn't stand it that people who needed this place couldn't afford it, and he was determined to, as he put it, 'keep on greeting and helping folks right here, even after I've gone on'."

"So I've called his son, and he's said you're welcome to join 'Sam's club', as he calls it. What that means is **the first $100,000 of your mom's care is paid for."**

The couple's eyes flew open as they stared incredulously at the administrator.
"What?", they both exclaimed. "How can that be?"
The administrator smiled. "I don't get it either, but if people ask, I'm just supposed to tell them this: **'Matthew 20:16'. That's it."**

"But mom's really sick. They think soon she'll be in hospice. **What happens if she dies before she uses all that money?"**

"Well, you're not going to believe this either." He paused, looking them straight in the eye as he continued. "Whatever money that's left will go wherever your mom wants it to go. Matthew 20:16 is the only guideline Sam gave."

The wife was thinking hard about this one. "You mean the gift's the same for someone who dies soon as for someone who lives here for years? It's wonderful, don't get me wrong, but **it somehow doesn't seem fair that Mom could really get more money than someone like that."**

The administrator reached in his desk drawer and handed them each a business card. One of Sam's business cards. "Turn it over", he told them. They did, and this is what they saw:

"And so it is, that many who are first now will be last then; and those who are last now will be first then."- *Matthew 20:16 (New Living Translation)*

* * * * * * * * * *

We, likethe humans we are, tend to focus on the times when we, like the vineyard workers who sweated and toiled all day, feel the 'down side' of 'unfair'. Sometimes we don't even notice (or pay attention to?) all the times when the 'unfairness' is so much more than 'fair' to us. We can become increasingly bitter with life....and in our relationship with God too.

Take some time to think, really think. Have there been times this week (month, year...) when you've received more than you thought you would?
When things have gone better than you thought they would?
Even those seemingly little things add up!
Let God touch you with those memories, and be blessed by them.

I found out later that Sam began life in Appalachia, in a poorest-of-the-poor family in the 'backwoods'. He was **determined to live out Matthew 20:16.**

How about us? **How can we pass that message on?** How can we, like Sam, help others focus on the blessings? **How can we say, with a Christ-given smile – oh, yeah, it's NOT fair, is it?"**

Reflections

What do you do when you feel like those workers who worked all day in the vineyard?

Reflections (continued)...

Do people tend to notice it more when they're like those workers....or more when they're like the ones hired at the end of the day, but paid the same? Why do you think this is?

What does 'fair' mean to you?

20

Handed Over

*Jesus, now well on the way to Jerusalem, took the Twelve off to the side of the road and said, "Listen to me carefully. **We are on our way** up to Jerusalem. When we get there, the Son of Man will be **betrayed** to the religious leaders and scholars. They will sentence him to death. They **will hand him over** to the Romans for mockery and torture and crucifixion. **On the third day he will be raised up alive**."*

- Matthew 20:17-19 (The Message Version)

*As Jesus was **on the way** to Jerusalem, he took the twelve disciples aside privately and told them what was going to happen to him. "When we get to Jerusalem," he said, "the Son of Man **will be betrayed** to the leading priests and the teachers of religious law. They will sentence him to die. Then they **will hand him over** to the Romans to be mocked, whipped, and crucified. But **on the third day he will be raised from the dead.**"*

- Matthew 20: 17-19 (New Revised Standard Version)

* * * * * * * * * *

It was a conversation I **overheard in an airport a long time ago**. Having recently flown east for my daughter's wedding, I remembered it as I sat waiting in the airport.

A young boy was flying 'unaccompanied'. No adult would be flying with him, so the airport gate agent was explaining to him the process of getting him **from the airport in a small city in Michigan to the one in an equally small city in Germany.**

There seemed to be many stops and plane changes this boy would have to negotiate, and **as the agent explained them to him, each step began with 'then you'll be handed over to......' or 'then they'll hand you over to...'.**

After the agent was finished, **she asked him if he understood**, if he had any questions. Clearly not too comfortable with the whole thing, he asked her, **"So why do I have to be 'handed over' all the time anyway?"**

Then came the agent's explanation and the boy's reply that I'll never forget:
"Why, honey, that's so if something happens to the plane, they'll know if you were on board or not."

Whoa! THAT got my attention! **How COULD she** say something like that to anyone, let alone a young boy?

He seemed to think a minute. Then his reply came: **"Well, I guess if Jesus got 'handed over' and He came out OK, I will too."**

* * * * * * * * * *

Handed over. Ever feel like that? Be honest now, don't you have days (or weeks, or...) where you feel like you're just being 'handed over' from one thing to another, from one job or chore to another? Ever wonder where it could all end?

Well, here's Jesus' answer, loud and clear. You'll end with Him. Forever.
His journey took Him all over the place. Cesarea, Jerusalem, Galilee, ...
Your journey will take you all over the place too. Home, work, school, perhaps even moving to a new home,.....

But if you travel with Jesus, one thing is certain.
Your last 'handing over' will land you...right in His arms.

No matter if you feel betrayed, mocked, even tortured and crucified...
Handed over.
That's right.
Jesus is right there with you, in the middle of all your times of being 'handed over'.
He's been there, done that. Oh, yeah.

Won't you begin today, and every day, by handing yourself over to Him?
You'll find a life strengthened by His incredible grace and peace.

Reflections

What does being 'handed over' mean to you?

How would you have answered the boy's question?

What does 'handing yourself over to Christ' mean in your life? Is it possible for you?

21

Priority Pricing

Then the mother of the sons of Zebedee came to him with her sons, and kneeling before him, she asked a favor of him.

And he said to her, "What do you want?" She said to him, **"Declare that these two sons of mine will sit, one at your right hand and one at your left, in your kingdom."**

But Jesus answered, **"You do not know what you are asking.** *Are you able to drink the cup that I am about to drink?" They said to him, "We are able."*

He said to them, "You will indeed drink my cup, but to sit at my right hand and at my left, this is not mine to grant, but it is for those for whom it has been prepared by my Father."

When the ten heard it, they were angry with the two brothers. But Jesus called them to him and said, "You know that the rulers of the Gentiles lord it over them, and their great ones are tyrants over them. It will not be so among you; but **whoever wishes to be great among you must be your servant,** *and whoever wishes to be first among you must be your slave; just as the* **Son of Man came not to be served but to serve, and to give his life a ransom for many."**

- Matthew 20: 20-28 (New Revised Standard Version)

It was about that time that the mother of the Zebedee brothers came with her two sons and knelt before Jesus with a request. "What do you want?", Jesus asked.

She said, **"Give your word that these two sons of mine will be awarded the highest places of honor in your kingdom,** *one at your right hand, and one at your left hand."*

Jesus responded, **"You have no idea what you're asking."** *And he said to James and John, "Are you capable of drinking the cup that I'm about to drink?"*

They said, "Sure, why not?"

Jesus said, "Come to think of it, you are *going to drink my cup. But as to awarding places of honor, that's not my business. My Father is taking care of that."*

When the ten others heard about this, they lost their tempers, thoroughly disgusted with the two brothers. So Jesus got them together to settle things down. He said, "You've observed how godless rulers throw their weight around, how quickly a little power goes to their heads. It's not going to be that way with you. **Whoever wants to be great must become a servant.** *Whoever wants to be first among you must be your slave. That* **is what the Son of Man has done. He came to serve, not be served – and then to give away his life in exchange for the many who are held hostage."**

- Matthew 20: 20-28 (The Message Version)

* * * * * * * * * *

The **district sales meeting** was in full swing. "It's priority pricing power!", the presenter declared. **"Say that with me: It's <u>priority pricing power!</u>"**

He went on to explain that advertised sale items (you know, like the 5 packages of index cards for a dollar, or those buy one, get one free offers) might seem small and unimportant. In reality, however, selecting them is a big priority, thus 'priority pricing <u>power</u>'!

He continued, **"Those 'little things' are what bring people in to see** the big things we really want them to buy!"

So **the most important thingwasn't the big, showy, seemingly important things**. It was the 'priority' items that fell at the bottom of most of our lists: paper clips, pens, paper, etc.! Those big things showcased in the store windows might <u>look</u> important, but it's marketing and sales of the everyday things that really attracts people and brings them in to seethe rest.

So the items with the biggest effect are the small ones we might not even notice - the everyday stuff.

Lately, many eyes have been on the failings of a local megachurch pastor who has been fired for inappropriate (and perhaps illegal) behavior. That's the 'big show'. **But what about the everyday people?** What about the folks who participate in that church?His family? Friends? Neighbors?

You see, Jesus is telling James, John, their mother, andus that **it's the everyday, the seemingly small and many times unnoticed, everyday servants who are great in God's kingdom.** This pastor, and those in positions like his, have much less power than we (or they) might think. Jesus is reminding us that worldly vision doesn't always match heavenly vision. In fact it seldom, if ever does!

It's really those everyday servants who are the greatest in God's eyes; they have (are you ready?) ….**Priority Servant Power!**

So go ahead, **be a paper clip** – share with others how knowing and following Christ helps you hold life together!

Go ahead, **be a pen** – let God write Kingdom news in and through you!

Go ahead, **be a sheet of paper** for Christ – let God write the Good News all over you for those you meet to read!

The 'Big News' IS the Good News of Christ, and <u>you</u> are God's everyday 'priority power servant'. It's <u>you</u> that will attract and lead others to the best news they'll ever hear – that Jesus Christ, the Son of the Living God, came to give His life that we would live our lives in His grace.

It's Priority Servant Power!

Feel it!Live it!Share it!

Reflections

How could people see you as God's 'paper clip'? Pen? Sheet of paper?

What does this message say to us when we're tempted to give people, events, and things more 'priority' than God would give them?

22

Obnoxious Faith

As Jesus and the disciples left the city of Jericho, a huge crowd followed behind. **Two blind men were sitting** *beside the road. When they heard that Jesus was coming that way,* **they began shouting, "Lord, Son of David, have mercy on us!"** **The crowd told them to be quiet, but they only shouted louder, "Lord, Son of David, have mercy on us!"** *Jesus stopped in the road and called, "What do you want me to do for you?" "Lord," they said, "We want to see!"* **Jesus felt sorry for them and touched their eyes. Instantly they could see! Then they followed him.**
— Matthew 20: 29-34 (New Living Translation)

As they were leaving Jericho, a huge crowd followed. Suddenly they came upon **two blind men sitting alongside the road.** *When they heard it was Jesus passing,* **they cried out, "Master, have mercy on us! Mercy, Son of David!"**
The crowd told them to be quiet, but they just kept at it, shouting even louder, *"Master, have mercy on us! Mercy, Son of David!"*
Jesus stopped and called over, "What do you want from me?"
They said, "Master, we want our eyes opened. We want to see!"
Deeply moved, **Jesus touched their eyes. They had their sight back that very instant, and joined the procession.**
— Matthew 20: 29-34 (The Message Version)

* * * * * * * * * *

"Mom!!"
Immersed in grocery store parking lot conversation with a friend, the woman ignored the first 'Mom!' coming from her little girl in the shopping cart.

"Mo-o-o-o-om!!" This little girl was NOT to be ignored!
'What now?', she thought. Having just come through the store, where her daughter seemed to beg for everything in sight, she wasn't too inclined to pay a lot of attention now.

"Momma! Look!!"
Exasperated, she turned to her daughter, fire in her eyes.
"WHAT? What do you WANT?"
"I want you to LOOK! At the bad man by our car!"

Oh my gosh! As she turned to look where her little girl was pointing, there was indeed a man trying to break into their car!

* * * * * * * * * *

I must admit, when I first heard the little girl's wail (having witnessed her begging for toys in the store), **I said to myself, 'what an obnoxious child!'.** I was glad she wasn't with me, and **certainly glad she wasn't going home with me!**

When she yelled a second time, I winced as her screech hit my eardrums. Her mom's 'WHAT?' echoed in my mind too.

But then reality hit as I too turned to see where she was pointing. The mom yelled, and the man ran as she dialed 911 on her cell phone. It was a good thing this little girl was so persistent!

Sometimes we pray for things that might seem strange to other people - maybe even impossible. **Sometimes people we know caution us to 'be quiet',** just as the crowd did in this Scripture reading. **Sometimes they wonder why we're praying at all.**

These men wanted to see. They knew Jesus could help them, could heal them. **We see their immediate persistence,** their refusal to let the crowd stop them from appealing to Jesus – **OK, their obnoxious faith in action!** It's the attention-getting scene. **But their persistence goes beyond that.** They 'followed him'; they 'joined the procession'. Why?

Maybe they knew that in their 'sometimes' world, Jesus was an 'always' Savior.
Maybe they learned that sticking to Jesus would mean more and more sight, more and more vision – Godly, eternal vision!

Maybe we could learn something from their persistence, their obnoxious faith. Never give up on Jesus – He'll never give up on you!
If you stick to Jesus, stay in prayer, in conversation with Him, **you'll be amazed to see more and more of God's purpose and vision for you.**

Just like these men, follow Jesus' example, His leading. Ask Him daily to increase your vision too! **Join His 'procession'!**

Reflections

In what ways does our culture/society pressure us to 'keep quiet' about our faith?

What are some ways in which we can be persistent about sharing our faith? Hint: think about special abilities and/or talents you have. How can you use them to share your faith?

What is the difference between "persistent" and "obnoxious"? Did your opinion of the little girl change when you found out what she was yelling about? If so, why do you think that is?

23

Feast Offerings

When they had come near Jerusalem and had reached Bethphage, at the Mount of Olives, Jesus sent two disciples, saying to them, "Go into the village ahead of you, and immediately you will find a donkey tied, and a colt with her; untie them and bring them to me. If anyone says anything to you, just say this, 'The Lord needs them.' And he will send them immediately. "

This took place to fulfill what had been spoken through the prophet, saying, "Tell the daughter of Zion, Look, your king is coming to you, humble, and mounted on a donkey, and on a colt, the foal of a donkey."

The disciples went and did as Jesus had directed them; they brought the donkey and the colt, and put their cloaks on them, and he sat on them. **A very large crowd spread their cloaks on the road, and others cut branches from the trees and spread them on the road.**

The crowds that went ahead of him and that followed were shouting, "Hosanna to the Son of David! Blessed is the one who comes in the name of the Lord! Hosanna in the highest heaven!"

When he entered Jerusalem, the whole city was in turmoil, asking, "Who is this?"

The crowds were saying, "This is the prophet Jesus from Nazareth in Galilee."

- Matthew 21: 1-11 (New Revised Standard Version)

As Jesus and the disciples approached Jerusalem, they came to the town of Bethphage on the Mount of Olives. Jesus sent two of them on ahead.

"Go into the village over there," he said, "and you will see a donkey tied there, with its colt beside it. Untie them and bring them here. If anyone asks what you are doing, just say, 'The Lord needs them,' and he will immediately send them."

This was done to fulfill the prophecy,

"Tell the people of Israel, 'Look, your King is coming to you. He is humble, riding on a donkey —even on a donkey's colt.' "

The two disciples did as Jesus said. They brought the animals to him and threw their garments over the colt, and he sat on it.

Most of the crowd spread their coats on the road ahead of Jesus, and others cut branches from the trees and spread them on the road.

He was in the center of the procession, and the crowds all around him were shouting, "Praise God for the Son of David! Bless the one who comes in the name of the Lord! Praise God in highest heaven!"

The entire city of Jerusalem was stirred as he entered. "Who is this?" they asked.

And the crowds replied, "It's Jesus, the prophet from Nazareth in Galilee."

- Matthew 21: 1-11 (New Living Translation)

* * * * * * * * *

"All are welcome!We're <u>THANKFUL</u> you're here!", the large, obviously children's group-made sign outside the church fellowship hall entrance proclaimed. Inside, the air fairly bubbled with excitement as plates and silverware clinked and laughter filled the air.

Suddenly, a ripple of silence rippled through the hustle and bustle. "Where's the pastor?" "I don't know." "Over there." "There's a WHAT?" "He brought WHAT?"

Into the now almost silent hall came a joyful young voice. "Oh boy, mister, come back, PLEASE! **I LOVE popcorn, and** (jumping excitedly up and down now) **you've got enough for the whole WORLD to share!"**

The man turned slowly around, pulling his cart with him. He had been just about to leave, sure that like most places, he wasn't really welcome here either. But the excitement of that little girl stopped him right in his tracks. What was that in his cart? Why, it looked like......**it was indeed.....what looked like a 50 pound bag of –popcorn!**

"**I didn't have anything else.** Usually we just go down by the river and make a fire. Then we all gather around and pop corn for Thanksgiving. **It's usually all we've got,** but this year with my bad leg and all I just can't walk that far. **And, well, I saw the sign, and..."**

No one seemed to know quite what to say, but the little girl never skipped a beat. Sensing his need to share, she bounced right up to him. "Well, you can't leave now, mister. How 'bout trading some ofyour popcorn for some of our turkey and stuff? We got pie, too....and ice cream!!" And with that, she bounced up to him and gave him a big hug around the knees!

That's how the whole 'turkey-and-popcorn' tradition began. One of the men in the church grabbed the church van keys. He and the 'popcorn man' set out to find his friends down by the river. They all came back for a wonderful Thanksgiving dinner together, but **the best part of the tradition came after the meal – started by, you guessed it – that same little girl.**

It came time to take the 'popcorn people' back. The problem was that a few of them were busy enthralling the kids with wonderful stories. **"No! No! They can't go yet!"** Up piped her voice again, **"We've got to have some river popcorn!** Can we go? They came to our house. Can't we go to theirs? We could pop corn – and hear more stories!!"

So they packaged up rolls, pie, and other goodies (that didn't need a refrigerator) and **trekked to the river.** There they found a group of folks huddled around a couple of fires. "Hey, Buddy! Got the popcorn? Who're all your new friends?" **For years to come they would all remember that Thanksgiving.** Oh, not so much the turkey, trimmings, pie, or even the ice cream, but popcorn and stories around fires down by the river.

This was the birth of the Jordan River Shelter, begun right around those fires that night, begun with one little girl's sparkling welcome, one little girl's overwhelming thanksgiving for popcorn and stories, and one little girl's love for an old man who thought he had nothing big to offer.

The truth is, he had so much more to offer than he could ever have dreamed, and in sharing it he gave those who welcomed him so much more to be thankful for than they could have ever imagined.

And his real name? "Well, honey," he told her, "My friends call me Buddy, most just call me Old Man, but **my mama, why she called me Joshua.**"

Her little mouth fell open. "**Why, mister, do you know what that means?** My Sunday School teacher said your name, **why it means.....it means....JESUS!!**"

* * * * * * * * * *

Yes, Jesus came to that churchThanksgiving dinner that year.
Not at all what they would have expected.

The following Sunday when they all sang:
"**Come, O long expected Jesus;** come to set your people free. From our sins and fears release us, Christ in Whom our rest shall be...." (Charles Wesley hymn, 1744), **there wasn't a dry eye in the place.**

Sometimes we feel that what we offer God, our 'feast-offering' in thanks for all God has given us, **isn't worth much.**
Sometimes we, like Joshua, turn back just short of offering it to God.
Sometimes we don't even bother at all.
Remember that, just like that popcorn and that little girl, God is absolutely thrilled with your offering of thanks. Absolutely.

Remember too, that **God offered Jesus – just for us. The biggest offering ever, and yet many turn back just short of accepting God's greatest gift. Some never bother at all.**

Come to the Feast at Christ's Table. Simply bring yourself – the best gift you can ever offer, and accept God's gift for you.

Reflections

Why would someone think they didn't have much to offer? What would you tell such a person?

Name three things you couldn't eat or buy that could be 'offered' at Thanksgiving. Why do you think each is important?

Why might someone argue with the statement, "Simply bring yourself – the best gift you can ever offer, and accept God's gift for you."?

24

Clean Focus

Jesus entered the Temple and began to drive out the merchants and their customers. He knocked over the tables *of the money changers and the stalls of those selling doves. He said, "The Scriptures declare, 'My Temple will be called a place of prayer,' but you have turned it into a den of thieves!"*

The blind and the lame came to him, and he healed them there in the Temple.

The leading priests and the teachers of religious law saw these wonderful miracles and heard even the children in the Temple shouting, "Praise God for the Son of David." But **the leaders were indignant. They asked Jesus, "Do you hear what these children are saying?"**

"Yes," Jesus replied. "Haven't you ever read the Scriptures? For they say, 'You have taught children and infants to give you praise.' " Then he returned to Bethany, where he stayed overnight.

- Matthew 21: 12-17 (New Living Translation)

Jesus went straight to the Temple and threw out everyone who had set up shop, buying and selling. He *kicked over the tables of loan sharks and the stalls of dove merchants. He quoted this text: "My house was designated a house of prayer; you have made it a hangout for thieves."*

Now there was room for the blind and crippled to get in. They came to Jesus and He healed them.

When the religious leaders saw the outrageous things He was doing, and heard all the children running and shouting through the Temple, 'Hosanna to David's Son!' **they were up in arms and took Him to task. "Do you hear what these children are saying?"**

Jesus said, "Yes, I hear them. And haven't you read in God's Word, 'From the mouths of children and babies I'll furnish a place of praise'?" Fed up, Jesus turned on His heel and left the city for Bethany, where He spent the night.-
Matthew 21: 12-17 (The Message Version)

* * * * * * * * *

It was when Santa moved that I first suspected it. The way he seemed to listen carefully. Very carefully. After waiting in line for what seemed like hours, my kids and I had finally made it.

We'd be the last to see Santa before he took a break. It had been my youngest son Dan who had insisted (as only he could). 'Santa in shades' was just too interesting. "I wanna see the cool Santa, that one, the one with the shaaaades."

The concept of long lines was above his two year old comprehension, but definitely not beyond his four year old sister. "We'll be here for hou-----rs!", she declared." (and not quietly either) So here we were.

Now that we were up close, I could tell she was intrigued by this rather different sort of Santa. Getting up close to Santa had definitely cooled two-year old Dan's enthusiasm, but four-year old Sandi was now very interested. So up she went, right up to Santa, where **she soon declared, "You can't see me, can you Santa?"**

Bless his heart, he never missed a beat. "Why no, sweetheart, but I can tell you're a real nice little girl. Want to come tell me what you want for Christmas?" So up she went. I'll never know what she whispered in his ear, but it made Santa cry.

Right there in the middle of the mall. Santa himself, crying. I started forward (you know, a mom thing), but he put his hand up and smiled at me. **"You got a real special little girl, ma'am, a real special child. She just made my Christmas."**

As Sandi scampered back to me, he called out a hearty, "Ho! Ho! Ho! Merry Christmas!" and began to get up from his chair....but no, his whole chair was moving! Sandi must have noticed the confused look on my face, because she explained it to me: **"Santa doesn't have any legs, but he's got a great big heart. I think he's got Jesus in there!"**

Santa's wife came out to see us. She shared with me how her husband **had lost his sight and his legs while serving in Vietnam years before.** "Kids, they have room for him.", she explained. "Doing this makes his whole year better. **He says kids don't have their hearts 'all junked up', he calls it; they have room for the real Spirit of Christmas.** Us grownups, well, just look around at all this shopping frenzy....."

It was right there in that mall I rededicated myself to working on cleaning my own 'moneychangers' out, out of my heart, because you know what? Unless I do, before long there's no room left for anything else.

If I fill my life and my heart with all the other 'stuff' (come on, it's easy to do, so easy you won't even notice you've got no heart-room until....), I won't even notice my own blindness, my own crippling. **It's when I work on cleaning out my 'junked-up heart' that I can claim my own blind spots, my own crippled parts – and present them to Christ for the healing only He can give.**

Oh yes, Jesus chased the buyers and sellers, the moneychangers, out of the Temple. He made room for the blind and crippled who desperately needed His healing touch. And so they came. And He healed them.

Your life is a temple, a testimony to what God can do in Christ – in and through you. You were created in the image of God. Your heart is indeed created to be a place of prayer.

Will you ask Christ.....will you let Him – help you chase your 'heart-junk' out?

Will you ask Him....will you let Christ – heal your blindness, your brokenness?

How about a little 'heart-cleaning'?

Reflections

If you were to guess, what do you think young Sandi said to Santa?

As we live our lives, we gather "heart-junk" each and every day. How can we work on cleaning it out so our vision of God is clearer, so we can see how God is calling and blessing us?

Take a few minutes (or more if you need it) to think of at least one piece of "heart-junk" that's clouding your life's vision or crippling your life journey. Now form a plan to get it out of your way. How will you begin to "work your plan"? Be sure you invite Christ into your plan – make it His!

25

Use It or Lose It!

*In the morning, when he returned to the city, he was hungry. And **seeing a fig tree by the side of the road, he went to it and found nothing at all on it but leaves.** Then he said to it, "May no fruit ever come from you again!" And the fig tree withered at once.*

*When the disciples saw it, **they were amazed, saying, "How did the fig tree wither at once?"***

*Jesus answered them, "Truly I tell you, if you have faith and do not doubt, not only will you do what has been done to the fig tree, but even if you say to this mountain, 'Be lifted up and thrown into the sea,' it will be done. **Whatever you ask for in prayer with faith, you will receive."***

- Matthew 21: 18-22 (New Revised Standard Version)

*Early the next morning, Jesus was returning to the city. He was hungry. Seeing a lone fig tree alongside the road, **he approached it anticipating a breakfast of figs. When he got to the tree, there was nothing but fig leaves.***

He said, "No more figs from this tree – ever!" The fig tree withered on the spot, a dry stick.

*The disciples saw it happen. They rubbed their eyes, saying, **"Did we really see this? A leafy tree one minute, a dry stick the next?"***

*But Jesus was matter-of-fact: "Yes – and if you embrace this kingdom life and don't doubt God, you'll not only do minor feats like I did to the fig tree, but also triumph over huge obstacles. This mountain, for instance, you'll tell, 'Go jump in the lake', and it will jump. **Absolutely everything, ranging from small to large, as you make it a part of your believing prayer, gets included as you lay hold of God."***

- Matthew 21: 18-22 (The Message Version)

* * * * * * * * * *

"Boy, am I glad that I'm not that fig tree!"

We'd started this retreat for spiritual renewal with the Scripture you see above. Seemed rather mysterious (OK, crazy) a selection to begin with to most of us, and as we gathered and waited for the retreat leader to show up, **it seemed to loom larger and larger on the board at the front of the room.**

What was the leader trying to say? Was it that we were too late? Was it, 'watch out, 'cause God's about to treat you like that fig tree'?

And the bottom line, really: Was I in the right place?

As I looked around the room, I began to think – what's the difference between figs and leaves? Just then our retreat leader arrived. **He took down the paper with the Scripture passage on it, but our collective 'Whew!' was short-lived.**

He reached into a cabinet and pulled out a basket full of (you guessed it) **figs. These figs were nestled in beautiful green leaves** – fig leaves, he told us.

"Don't these leaves look good?", he asked us. Now having been around a while, none of us answered – we just waited. So did he. Then he asked a question....

"So, which would you want for breakfast: leaves, or figs?"

Several voices ventured together – "Figs."

"But these leaves," he countered, **"They're beautiful.** All green and shiny. They look so nice..."

"Oh yea, like they'd be tasty! Oh, sorry, I didn't mean to...." The hospitality host had responded without thinking. I hadn't even noticed him busily bringing in more refreshments.

"No problem. In fact, folks, I want you all to **meet Rick. These leaves and figs came from his tree. Thanks, Rick."** Rick blushed and went back to arranging snacks.

"I wonder what these leaves will look like at the end of our four days here?" Our leader looked around the circle. **"I wonder what the figs will look like."**

"Well", one brave soul spoke up, "The leaves will wither. They won't look so good, but I don't get it, because the figs, well, they'll rot and mold. That's just nasty!"

With that, the retreat **leader reached in his pocket and pulled out his pocket knife,** grabbed a fig from the bowl, and sliced it in half. "You know, when this retreat's over, **I'll take these figs and leaves and throw them in my compost pile.** The leaves, well, you're right, they'll crumble and rot. So will the figs. **But the seeds** inside these figs, now that's another story."

He looked around the circle, meeting each of our eyes. Then he turned to Rick. **"Hey Rick, just one more thing......thanks for the tree.** It's about this tall now!"

Rick looked up, blushing again. "Why, you're welcome. **It was nothing, really. That's just the way it works. I get those little fig tree sprouts in my compost bin** all the time – every spring. Glad you like them!" And off Rick went.

Then we got down to business. **"I wonder how many of you are down to just leaves?** You know, lookin' OK, but with no fruit in your lives..... I wonder how many of you've been so busy tending the leaves you've forgotten to feed the fruit. **Maybe you haven't even noticed – you're all leaves."**

"And I wonder **how many of you have just one piece of fruit in your life,** and it's withering, about to fall and die. **You haven't used it, and now you're losing it."**

"And I wonder how many of you are asking yourself right now – how did I get this way? **How did this happen?"**

None of us dared to look around. We were too busy looking inside. Fig-hunting.

"Jesus found no figs on that tree. Only leaves. Use it or lose it." Silence.

"Maybe you think there aren't any figs, any fruit, on your spiritual 'tree' either. But listen again: *'Absolutely everything, ranging from small to large, as you make it a part of your believing prayer, gets included as you lay hold of God.'"*

More silence.

"**When's the last time you 'laid hold of God'?** Too busy, huh? Use it, or risk losing it. **Remember the woman who just touched the fringe of Jesus' robe?** Just the fringe.
(Luke 8: 43-48)

"**She laid hold of God through Jesus – with all she had left** – and she was healed. Her fruit restored. Whole again. Resurrection power. Ever wonder how many seeds of faith she planted after that? **How many spiritual trees grew from that one encounter?**"

"I want you to **lay hold of God. Right now.** Because even if you can't see the fruit, God can. It's there. Or **maybe you need a whole new tree** to grow in your spirit – maybe your old one's all withered and dead, nothing but a dry stick.

You didn't use it, and now you've lost it. Time to give up? No way! **Lay hold of God in prayer. Allow God to sprout those long forgotten fig-seeds in you.**

Open yourself to the power of the Holy Spirit – and **let Christ truly be born...in you!**

Reflections

What did you think of when you read the words, "...lay hold of God."? What picture came to your mind?

What would the "life-equivalent" of Rick's compost pile be? Forgotten dreams? Broken relationships?

How could "new seeds" sprout from that kind of "compost pile"?

What does the phrase "Use it or lose it" mean to you – physically? Mentally? Spiritually?

26

Rights!

*When Jesus returned to the Temple and began teaching, the leading priests and other leaders came up to him. They demanded, "**By whose authority** did you drive out the merchants from the Temple? Who gave you such authority?"*

*"I'll tell you who gave me the authority to do these things if you answer one question," Jesus replied."**Did John's baptism come from heaven or was it merely human?**"*

*They talked it over among themselves. "**If we say it was from heaven**, he will ask why we didn't believe him.But **if we say it was merely human**, we'll be mobbed, because the people think he was a prophet."*

*So they finally **replied, "We don't know."** And Jesus responded, "Then I won't answer your question either.*
— Matthew 21:23-27 (New Living Translation)

Then he was back in the temple, teaching. The high priests and leaders of the people came up and demanded, "Show us your credentials. Who authorized you to teach here?"

*Jesus responded, "First let me ask you a question. You answer my question and I'll answer yours. **About the baptism of John – who authorized it: heaven, or humans?**"*

*__They were on the spot and they knew it.__ They pulled back into a huddle and whispered, "**If we say 'heaven'**, he'll ask us why we didn't believe him; **if we say 'humans'**, we're up against it with the people because they all hold john up as a prophet."*

*They decided to concede that round to Jesus. "**We don't know," they answered.** Jesus said, "Then neither will I answer your question."*

- Matthew 21: 23-27 (The Message Version)

* * * * * * * * * *

"Hey, Jimmy, is there really a Santa?"
Wow. Why couldn't his little brother just ask mom or dad?

"Jimmy, I mean it. Is Santa real? Some of the kids in my class at school, they say I'm a big baby 'cause I still believe in Santa."

What to say? Well, **if he told Brad there wasn't a Santa**, then he'd think he'd been lied to (not so far from the truth, but......). Nope, Jimmy could smell big trouble with that approach, but...... **if he told Brad there was a Santa**, well, Brad could spot a lie a mile away. He'd know Jimmy was lying, and then he'd be in trouble anyway......what to DO?

"Hey Jimmy, whatd'ya think, hmmm?"
"OK, Brad," Jimmy began. Then he had a thought. **"Hey, Brad, why do you want to know?"** A frown instantly crossed his little brother's face.

"Well, I've got a right to know, that's why! Who really comes at Christmas? I mean, is it Jesus like they say in church, or is it Santa like other people say?"

Jimmy looked around. Rats! No mom or dad in sight! **"Well, I don't know. Let me think about it."**

Brad was ready – he was a smart little boy! **"Oh, I get it. But I can tell the answer, 'cause I see how you talk to your friends. You never talk about Santa, or Jesus either. Never."** And he walked away, thinking hard.

* * * * * * * * * *

So, who is it that has 'Christmas authority'?

Could it be Christmas without Santa? Would it?

Here's another question (you knew this was coming).
Could it be Christmas without Jesus? Would it?

Who has the authority to decide? Is it a 'human-thing'? Or is it a 'God-thing'?
What would happen if we decided that it's Santa that really makes it Christmas?

Well, in the middle of all that, **like little Brad says, we "have a right to know". And God HAS let us know. Plainly. Jesus, God's Son, is what 'Christ-mas' is all about...to God.**

But **here's the glitch. We DO get to decide.** God has given us each free will, the 'right' to choose 'what it's all about'!

What would Brad think if he based his decision on watching you and I, on listening to us?
Do we spend as much time in spiritual pursuits, preparing our hearts to celebrate the eternal gift of Jesus during the Christmas season as we spend shopping, wrapping, hurrying and scurrying?
Who/What do we talk about with <u>our</u> friends?

God is waiting for you to choose to spend time with him. Will you let God fill your heart – with, well, 'whatever', or will it be the incredible gift of Jesus?

Brad's got it! **We have rights! God gives us the right to choose!** Will our lives be based on the temporary (although many times fun and rewarding) 'stuff', or will our priority be Christ – God's Gift of eternal Life?

Reflections

What DO people have a "right to know"? For each thing you think of, WHY is this?

What would Brad think if he watched you to learn what was important? Would it be what you'd want him to see and learn from?

What examples did you watch and learn from as you grew up? What did they teach you? Have you kept those lessons, and if so, how have they changed over time?

What would you say to Brad?

27

What's My Line?

"What do you think? A man had two sons; he went to the first and said, 'Son, go and work in the vineyard today.'

He answered, 'I will not'; but later he changed his mind and went.

*The father went to the second and said the same; and **he answered, 'I go, sir'; but he did not go.***

Which of the two did the will of his father?" They said, "The first." *Jesus said to them, "Truly I tell you, the tax collectors and the prostitutes are going into the kingdom of God ahead of you.*

*For John came to you in the way of righteousness and you did not believe him, but the tax collectors and the prostitutes believed him; and **even after you saw it, you did not change your minds and believe him.***
- Matthew 21: 28-32 (New Revised Standard Version)

*"Tell me what you think about this story: A man had two sons. He went up to the first and said, 'Son, go out for the day and work in the vineyard.' **The son answered, 'I don't want to.' Later on he thought better of it and went.***

*"The father gave the same command to the **second son. He answered, 'Sure, glad to.' But he never went.** **"Which of the two sons did what the father asked?"***

They said, "The first."

*Jesus said, "Yes, and I tell you that crooks and whores are going to precede you into God's kingdom. John came to you showing you the right road. You turned up your noses at him, but the crooks and whores believed him. **Even when you saw their changed lives, you didn't care enough to change and believe him.***
- Matthew 21: 28-32 (The Message Version)

* * * * * * * * * *

The woman walked over to my table holding one of our church postcards in her hand. "Can I ask you something? **It may be a dumb question, but.....your church, it says 'Disciples of Christ'. Is that the same thing as regular Christians**, I mean, you know, I see Welcome Table <u>Christian</u> Church, but I'm wondering if this 'Disciples of Christ' **makes it different from all those other so-called Christian people and churches** I've come across."

"Well," I asked her, **"Can you tell me a bit about your experiences** with Christians and Christian churches? Then maybe I can give you a better answer."

"**Well, they seem to talk a good talk** – I can't disagree with most of what they say, but that **seems to be all it is most times – talk.** Don't get me wrong, I mean, I'm not expecting perfect, but lots of times they'll promise stuff or spout all these great sounding guidelines for living. Then, well, **they just seem to have awfully convenient memories.....or maybe they don't really believe what they're saying."**

I could understand her confusion. Been there, seen that. Among all the 'Christians' she'd come in contact with, **she was trying to figure out what was genuine,** what was worth paying attention to, and/ or what was worth risking herself to explore more. What she'd seen wasn't too promising, but I was glad to see she was still willing to ask the questions.

"Well," she continued, **"I saw this great invitation card of yours with the empty toilet paper roll on it,** and I thought, **'yep, that's how I'm starting to feel about this whole church thing'.** Then **I remembered** your name. **I've seen** you all down at Hughes Station (that place for folks who need help), and **I saw** you in the paper a while back, fixing those peoples' homes. And **a friend of mine, she's doing some stuff with your church too.** She's been hurt real bad by a church, and I figure **there must be something to this 'Disciples' thing** if she's coming. I figure **if she's said a big fat 'NO' to church and she's coming, maybe I could too.** So how are these 'Disciples' different?"

So we talked. **We talked about Christ's real-world welcome** and the ministry of Welcome Table Christian Church. We talked **about Disciples of Christ as a bunch of real people living and struggling in a very real world.** She shared her own faith journey – her 'plains, mountains and hurdles', as she put it. Good conversation. After she left, I marveled at God's ability to reach so many different people in so many different ways, and thanked God for touching her and opening her up just a bit more to the realities and exciting possibilities of life as a true disciple of Christ.

She's seen and met many examples of the 'second son' in Jesus' story.
I prayed that she'd meet more and more examples of the 'first son'.

My spirit was warmed that she'd found some of those living examples in the people and ministry of Welcome Table Christian Church as we struggle to 'walk the talk' of discipleship to Christ.

What IS our 'line'? Will we merely talk it, or are we striving and struggling to walk it? I found myself praying that Christ would be born in her everyday life in real and authentic ways.

There are many like her. You've probably met at least one today. Maybe you identify with her struggle. **Maybe it's you.** No matter, you are welcome. **All are welcome. Today. Tomorrow. Always.**

Come to Christ's Table.
Let Him be born again, maybe even for the first time – in you, the real you.

Reflections

What kind of "lines" have you heard from churches and those calling themselves "Christians" in the past?

How did they make you feel?

Did the words turn out to match the actions?

What are some meaningful ways a Christian who "walks their talk" would answer the question, "What's YOUR line?" How would you be able to tell if they were genuine and authentic in their trying to live out that identity?

How are you doing with that?

28

The Christmas Stone

"Now listen to this story. A certain landowner planted a vineyard, built a wall around it, dug a pit for pressing out the grape juice, and built a lookout tower. Then he leased the vineyard to tenant farmers and moved to another country.

*"At the time of the grape harvest he sent his servants to collect his share of the crop.But the **farmers grabbed his servants, beat one, killed one, and stoned another.***

*"So the **landowner sent a larger group of his servants to collect for him, but the results were the same.***

*"**Finally, the owner sent his son**, thinking, 'Surely they will respect my son.'"But when the farmers saw his son coming, they said to one another, 'Here comes the heir to this estate. Come on, let's kill him and get the estate for ourselves!'**So they grabbed him, took him out of the vineyard, and murdered him.***

"When the owner of the vineyard returns," Jesus asked, "what do you think he will do to those farmers?"

"The religious leaders replied, "He will put the wicked men to a horrible death and lease the vineyard to others who will give him his share of the crop after each harvest."

*"Then Jesus asked them, "**Didn't you ever read this in the Scriptures? 'The stone rejected by the builders has now become the cornerstone.** This is the Lord's doing, and it is marvelous to see.' What I mean is that the Kingdom of God will be taken away from you and given to a nation that will produce the proper fruit.Anyone who stumbles over that stone will be broken to pieces, and it will crush anyone on whom it falls. "*

*When the leading priests and Pharisees heard Jesus, **they realized he was pointing at them–that they were the farmers in his story.** They wanted to arrest him, but they were afraid to try because the crowds considered Jesus to be a prophet.*

- Matthew 21: 33-46 (New Living Translation)

* * * * * * * * *

"You don't understand. **It was when my son, my SON, told me about Jesus that I finally listened,** really listened, and understood.**A guy I worked with tried to show me.** When I asked why he treated people the way he did, he, well, he flat-out told me it was because he was a follower of Jesus. Well, I told the boss he was trying to get me to believe, to go to his church. That was against the rules, so I got him fired. Then I got promoted and transferred. **I was new in town,so one of my bosses invited me to go to a Christmas event at her church.** I reported her, and she lost her job too. Soon I got promoted again.

"**Then my son, a senior in high school, interviewed me** fora 'success in business' article for his school paper. **He wanted to know about my climb up the corporate ladder.** As I shared with him what I thought was a teaching on what not to do in business (share your faith), he stared, open-mouthed. **'I understand perfectly,' he finally said. 'You rejected the Cornerstone.** God sent the first guy to show you Jesus. He just answered you honestly when you asked, Dad. You know that. And that boss. Come on, Dad. You were new in town and it was Christmas. Wow. Let me show you.' And with that, **he reached in his book bag and pulled out his Bible.**"

"**I didn't even know my son owned a Bible**, let alone read one, but he opened it right up and read that 'Cornerstone' story. Then came the real kicker. He looked me right in the eye and asked. Straight up. **'Dad,' he said, 'I'm asking you to come to church with me. Will you?**"

"**So that's why I'm here tonight.** I want to know my son, and I want to know why he wants me to know God's Son so much." He sat down, mystified at why he'd responded to the pastor's open invitation for guests to share why they'd come. As he glanced sideways at his son, he noticed **two things he'd never seen – tears in his son's eyes and a wonderful smile on his face.**

After worship, his son had another surprise. **"Hey dad, I want you to meet Chet.** He's the guy who invited me here last year. Thisis where I always go on Wednesday nights. Chet, meet my dad. **Oh, and this is Chet's mom."**

As he looked into Chet's mom's face, he felt as if a fist had slammed into the pit of his stomach. It couldn't be! "Hello, Bob. Good to see you again. Merry Christmas. Good to see you....here." She looked as shocked to see him as he was to see her. Why, **it'd been a couple of years since he'd turned her in for that invitation to the church Christmas event.**So whyshe was smiling? "You know, **you've got quite a son here. He's sure proud of you and all you've done..."** She hesitated.

He took a deep breath. **"Son, I want you to know that this lady is the boss I told you about.** What I did cost her herjob."

"Oh, I know that," his son answered with a smile. **"Now she owns another company** – in fact, they're your main competition. They've offered me a job when I graduate, even promised to help me with college. Isn't that great?"

* * * * * * * * *

So here's the question: Christmas has given us that Cornerstone, Jesus the Christ. Will we build with it? What will we build? How? When?

Each day gives us new grace, new opportunities to recognize Jesus at work in our lives, being born in new and sometimes surprising ways. Yes, like the dad in the story above, many times we waste those God-given opportunities. But here's the amazing thing about God: God never gives up. God was willing not only to send Jesus, but to give Him completely – for us. And each time we fail to see,… each time we see but fail to claim,… each time we see, claim, and fail to live our faith,….God presents Christ to us yet again!

So again, **what will we do this time?** I pray for you, and for myself, that we'll see, recognize, and live our faith, allowing God to take us to new, amazingly grace-filled new places on our journey of faith.

Reflections

Why do you think Bob reacted so strongly to those two people he "turned in", who lost their jobs?

What does the fact that Bob didn't know his son was involved in a youth group and going to church tell you about his life's priorities?

Is Jesus, the "Christmas Stone" (or Cornerstone – see Ephesians 2: 19-22) a foundation for you? If so, what are you building on it? If not, what do you think people who claim Christ as their foundation should be building?

29

Dress Code

*Once again Jesus used stories to teach the people: "The kingdom of heaven is like what happened when a **king gave a wedding banquet for his son.** The king **sent some servants to tell the invited guests to come to the banquet, but the guests refused.** He sent other servants to say to the guests, 'The banquet is ready! My cattle and prize calves have all been prepared. Everything is ready. Come to the banquet!'*

*"But **the guests did not pay any attention.** Some of them left for their farms, and some went to their places of business. Others **grabbed the servants, then beat them up and killed them.***

*"This made the king so furious that he sent an army to kill those murderers and burn down their city. Then he said to the servants, 'It is time for the wedding banquet, and the invited guests don't deserve to come. **Go out to the street corners and tell everyone you meet to come to the banquet.'***

*"They went out on the streets and **brought in everyone they could find, good and bad alike.** And the banquet room was filled with guests.*

*"When the king went in to meet the guests, **he found that one of them wasn't wearing the right clothes for the wedding. The king asked, "Friend, why didn't you wear proper clothes for the wedding?"** But the guest had no excuse. So the king gave orders for that person to be tied hand and foot and to be thrown outside into the dark. That's where people will cry and grit their teeth in pain. Many are invited, but only a few are chosen."*

- Matthew 22: 1-14 (Contemporary English Version)

* * * * * * * * * *

She'd planned her wedding for months (OK, years). Everything looked great. The church was beautiful. The hall was awesome. She'd been able to get the caterer she'd always wanted, and the smells from the kitchen almost made her want to just go eat first...almost.

But then she remembered - **yesterday her brothers had this huge fight.** Neither would come if the other was going to be there. The week before, her **dad had dropped a bombshell** on the family. He'd 'found someone else' and was moving out – the next day. **He didn't think he should be at the wedding.**

The idea had come her when she got up in church to read the Scripture lesson the Sunday before. It was out of her mouth before she knew it! As she looked around the church which would be decorated for her wedding in 6 days, the tears came. And Sue invited them all to come to her wedding. **'Bring all your friends', she'd said.** She turned to leave the podium. Then her face lit up and she stepped back to the microphone, a big grin on her face. **"Hey, bring anyone you know who could use some good food and a good time!"**

Her best friend stepped into the bride's dressing room. **"Sue, you're just NOT going to believe this!** This place is crammed with people! The ushers are even opening the balcony!" Sue peeked out to see. Wow! She'd only invited 100 people, but a full church meant over...200! "How will we feed all these people?" Sue was worried now. Her best friend started to laugh. "Oh, don't worry, the caterer's all overthis one. When she heard the story, well, let's just say she's determined this is going to be the BEST wedding feast ever!"

Back in the kitchen, a man wandered in. "This the place for the wedding?", he asked. Becky, one of the servers, looked him up and down. Oh boy. "Yea, I know," he nodded. "I'm not exactly dressed for it, am I?" **Becky noted his frayed, dirty jacket and faded jeans.** "Can I ....can I maybe give you a ride home real quick so you can change clothes?"As heturned and started to leave, an awful realization came to her. "Sir? Is that all the clothes you have? I mean...."

"Yes, little lady, I'm sorry to say. It's just, just that I heard about your bride, and, well.....**nothing should keep a daddy from his little girl's big day. No sirree, nothing. I missed my daughter's wedding – in Vietnam, I was. Can't get that back, nope, I sure can't.** Now she's gone. Cancer got her last year. If my bein' here's any help, well, OK. But if I'm not dressed good enough, well maybe I can help with the trash or something, you think?"

Becky had an idea. "Sir, would you wait right here a minute? I want you to meet someone." That was how 'Bones' (he'd been a medic in Vietnam) met Sue. The tux meant for Sue's dad was a little big, but it was OK,and after the groomsmen and bridesmaids got done trimming his hair and generally spoiling him, 'Mr. Bones' cut a pretty sharp image walking Sue down that aisle.

Right before they walked into the church, Bones turned to Sue. **"You know, girlie, I figure you've dressed my heart up big enough to last my whole life!"** And in they went.

* * * * * * * * * *

So why <u>didn't</u> **the guest have the proper clothing** for the King's wedding feast? We so often either overlook this little part of the story or **we say something like, 'Wow, that's not fair!** Just because he didn't have the right clothes he goes to hell?'

In the tradition of Jesus' time, weddings were usually held at the home of the groom's family. Additionally, if needed, **the groom's family would even provide appropriate clothing for guests!**

Given that fact, what's going on here...really? **Jesus says the guest 'had no excuse'.** So it wasn't that he didn't have the proper clothes, needed to go home and get them, or...whatever. No. He 'had no excuse'. The wedding wasn't important enough for him to dress appropriately, and he probably refused the clothing offered by the groom's family as well. **It wasn't so much his appearance,** but his heart and its priorities. If the invitation had been important enough, he would have taken advantage of the king's concern for his wardrobe needs.

God invites us each day to the 'Good News' banquet. The gift of Jesus Christ is worth celebrating each and every day! Do we 'dress' appropriately for this awesome every day grace-banquet? **I'm not talking about our physical clothing here.** Do we open our hearts, minds, and lives so that God can 'dress us up' with grace? Do we then show our thankfulness for God's banquet invitation in how we live each day? **You see, God's 'dress code'**

asks us to accept the robes of grace and the occasional (OK, often) 'trimming' we need to live in line with the gift of Jesus Christ.

Are we willing, like Bones, to open ourselves to being 'dressed' by God?

Reflections

How are physical clothes different from spiritual clothes? What does each say about us?

What would a "robe of grace" be like? How would you describe God's "dress code"?

Who do you most identify with in this story? Least identify with? Why do you think this is?

30

Whose IS It?

Then the Pharisees went and plotted to entrap him in what he said. So they sent their disciples to him, along with the Herodians, saying, "Teacher, we know that you are sincere, and teach the way of God in accordance with truth, and show deference to no one; for you do not regard people with partiality.Tell us, then, what you think. **Is it lawful to pay taxes to the emperor, or not?"**

But Jesus, aware of their malice, said, "Why are you putting me to the test, you hypocrites? **Show me the coin** *used for the tax." And they brought him a denarius.*

Then he said to them, **"Whose head is this, and whose title?"**

They answered, **"The emperor's."** *Then he said to them,* **"Give therefore to the emperor the things that are the emperor's, and to God the things that are God's."**

When they heard this, they were amazed; and they left him and went away.

- Matthew 22: 15-22 (New Revised Standard Version)

That's when the Pharisees plotted a way to trap him into saying something damaging. They sent their disciples, with a few of Herod's followers mixed in, to ask, "Teacher, we know you have integrity, teach the way of God accurately, are indifferent to popular opinion, and I pander to your students. So **tell us honestly: Is it right to pay taxes to Caesar or not?"**

Jesus knew they were up to no good. He said, "Why are you playing these games with me? Why are you trying to trap me? **Do you have a coin? Let me see it."**

They handed him a silver piece.

"This engraving – who does it look like? And whose name is on it?"

They said, "Caesar."

"Then give Caesar what is his, and give God what is his."

The Pharisees were speechless. They went off shaking their heads.

- Matthew 22: 15-22 (The Message Version)

* * * * * * * * * *

It was an interesting discussion. The **sermon that morning had been about....tithing.** Titled "Give God What's God's", it had been a frank look at what really does belong to God and what we were supposed to do with what God gave us.

Tara turned to her friend, a frown on her face. **"So Mary, what do you think of that sermon. Pretty far out, huh?** I mean, the church should be grateful for what we give, don't you think? What I mean is, **it's ours, right? We earned it**, so who's the pastor think he is, telling us what to do with it?"

Marythought a minute. **What should she say? A pastor's daughter**, she'd just returned to church after a fifteen year absence.Mary knew the financial realities of church. Honestly, she knew too much of the realities of 'church'. But something in whatTara said had hit a nerve,had touchedmemories of what her mother taught her so many years ago. **"Tara, I wonder, how much IS ours, really?"**

Tara's eyebrows shot up, then down as she frowned in concentration. "Well, I guess I can see that the **mountains and oceans and stuff like that belongs to God, but..."**

An inspiration flashed through Mary's mind. **"What about lakes that people make, like that waterski park down south?** And how about, well, Six Flags amusement park – you know, the rides and everything?"

Tara's eyes narrowed in concentration. "Well......**people made those**, so...."

"But what did they make them FROM? I mean the metal, the plastic, all that – where did the ingredients come from? Nature, right?" **Mary was finding herself rethinking** her own giving now...

Tara's eyes opened in surprise. **"I never thought about it like that.** If God made it in the first place; and God created us in the first place too.....Well, God created it all for us to enjoy and use. Kind of like lending it to us, I mean after we're gone, whatever's left in whatever shape it is goes to the next generation, right?" She laughed. "They always say, 'You can't take it with you', don't they?"

Now Mary was deep in thought too, thinking about the $5 she could 'spare' for the offering that morning. Thinking about the great promotion she'd just received at work. Thinking about the new car, new furniture, and new wardrobe she had planned. Could God be working on her, creating a 'new spirit' in her as well?

"Tara, you know what I just realized? **I just got a promotion at work** that I've been working so long for..."

A smile lit Tara's face. "Wow! **Congratulations!"**

Mary hesitated, but just for a second. "Yeah, well **I was in the middle of congratulating myself**, you know, for working so hard, for getting it all together, for, well, everything. Then it dawned on me. God gave me all the gifts, all the talent to get where I am. **Sure, I worked hard.** Sure, I used those talents. But it was God who planted the seeds in me. God. Just like we were talking about nature and Six Flags."

Now Tara looked confused. **"So what does it all mean?** If it's all God's, then are you saying we should give it all to God? But then what would we live on?"

"No, Tara, what I'm saying is **like that place where those guys ask Jesus about paying taxes**, you know, and He tells them to give God what's God's and the emperor what's his. If everything really ultimately belongs to God, then what? **I think there's different ways of 'giving it all to God'.** Like there's giving God the credit, being thankful for all the talents and gifts God's given us, thanking Him for sticking by us, for giving us Jesus. When I think about it that way, giving ten percent (that tithe thing) seems so small. Ten percent to help the church community work together to spread God's Good News...that's not so much. Ten percent to help us grow our faith, to be a stronger witness for Christ, to .....OK, you can stop me; now I'm preaching!"

Both women suddenly burst into laughter. "Preacher's daughter, oh yeah, I can see it now! But really, Mary, you're right. You've really helped me see some things."

"Tara, you know what? I'm going to call my mom. All those years of hearing her preach. Now she's retired. She's going to love this!"

"You know, Mary, **I just thought of something. It's not just ten percent of our money.** If it's God who gave us our talents and all that, shouldn't we give at least ten percent of that back to God too? I mean, **we could have FUN doing that!** I'm a school librarian, and our church library's a MESS! I've seen some really good stuff we could get, and I know where we can get a couple of computers and some great Bible software for that new kids' workshop-style Sunday school. Oh yeah, **this is going to be great – are you in with me?"**

What could Mary say? "Well, I'm a bookkeeper, and I could find out what money the church has. Maybe one of the things I could do to celebrate my new promotion would be to help buy that stuff for the kids! **With your tithe and mine together, God can do great things right here!** Sue's right over there; she heads up the new Sunday school. Let's go talk her!"

And that's how the new church library and kids' Sunday computer workshop began.

Reflections

Let Mary and Tara speak to you. With them, look honestly at your gifts and talents, your resources. What really is God's? Whose name is on your life?

Has this story invited you to think differently about "what's God's"? If so, how?

31

Live Power!

*"That same day some **Sadducees stepped forward–a group of Jews who say there is no resurrection after death.** They posed this question:"Teacher, Moses said, 'If a man dies without children, his brother should marry the widow and have a child who will be the brother's heir.'*

Well, there were seven brothers. The oldest married and then died without children, so the second brother married the widow.This brother also died without children, and the wife was married to the next brother, and so on until she had been the wife of each of them.And then she also died.So tell us, whose wife will she be in the resurrection? For she was the wife of all seven of them!"

*Jesus replied, "Your problem is that you don't know the Scriptures, and **you don't know the power of God.For when the dead rise, they won't be married. They will be like the angels in heaven.**But now, as to whether there will be a resurrection of the dead–haven't you ever read about this in the Scriptures? Long after Abraham, Isaac, and Jacob had died, **God said,'I am** the God of Abraham, the God of Isaac, and the God of Jacob.' So **he is the God of the living, not the dead."***

When the crowds heard him, they were impressed with his teaching.

- Matthew 22: 23-33 (New Living Translation)

*That same day, **Sadducees approached him. This is the party that denies any possibility of resurrection.** They asked, "Teacher, Moses said that if a man dies childless, his brother is obligated to marry his widow and get her with child. Here's a case where there were seven brothers. The first brother married and died, leaving no child, and his wife passed to his brother. The second brother also left her childless, then the third – and on and on, all seven. Eventually the wife died. Now here's our question. At the resurrection, whose wife is she? She was a wife to each of them."*

*Jesus answered, "You're off base on two counts: **You don't know your Bibles, and you don't know how God works. At the resurrection, we're beyond marriage.** As with the angels, all our ecstasies and intimacies then willbe with God. And regarding your speculation on whether the dead are raised or not, don't you read your Bibles? The grammar is clear: **God says, 'I am – not was** – the God of Abraham, the God of Isaac, the God of Jacob.' **The living God defines himself not as the God of the dead, but of the living."** Hearing this exchange the crowd was much impressed.*

- Matthew 22: 23-33 (The Message Version)

* * * * * * * * * *

"Grandma's dead, honey." With those words, I expected to see sadness, and probably tears. What I never expected was the bright smile that appeared on the little girl's face. **"Oh no, Dad, she's alive!"** What a strange response.

"No, sweetie, you don't understand. Grandma just died. She's dead. Now we know she's been sick for a long time, right?" **Curls bounced as the girl nodded, still smiling.** I could tell Dad was getting a bit embarrassed at this odd response. People in the hospital waiting area were beginning to look at them in odd ways. Dad continued, hoping Maisy would understand soon. **"So, Maisy, now we're going to plan grandma's funeral,** her special going away worship time."

"But DAD!" About to scold her, that smile stopped him. **Why WAS she still smiling?** "What, honey?"

"Dad, don't you read the BIBLE? I do, and so I know that grandma's not dead – she's alive like crazy! **If God IS, then grandma IS too! She's got God's LIVE POWER!** Can we have a party for her after her special church time? 'Cause Daddy, grandma knows Jesus, and this is her first birthday that she gets to hug Him – isn't that great, Daddy? Grandma's in God's LIVE POWER!!"

Now **how do you answer that?** It was the most amazing thing. People started clapping in that waiting room. First one. Then a couple. Soon applause fairly rang through the room and out into the hall. People looked in to see what the excitement was, and little Maisy told them.

She said, **"My grandma's gone home to God. She's having a Live Power party – right now, and Jesus is right there with her! Isn't that just the best thing you ever heard?"**

* * * * * * * * * *

It's amazing how God brings such powerful life from what we see as death, isn't it? Problem is, it's not always that easy to see the life, because we're busy looking at the death. But it's there, just like little Maisy in that waiting room with her dad.

All of us experience 'little deaths' in our lives. Isn't it good that we worship a Living God, a God who brings new life?

I met Maisy and her dad in a hospital waiting room. **Her grandma had been through three wars and three husbands** (all killed in combat). Dad really was thinking about which one would meet her in heaven. **Who could he tell Maisy was 'dancing with grandma in heaven'?** It turns out, it didn't matter to Maisy. Jesus was what mattered to her. A party with the Living God was what mattered to her. The rest was just, well, details. Maisy just rejoiced in God's 'LIVE POWER!'.

What if we, like Maisy, could focus on the power of the Living God we worship? Oh sure, we have to notice and deal with living in this world – all the 'details' of daily living. But could it be that we get so hung up in the details that they consume our focus, that they become the reason we live each day?

Could it be that, like the Pharisees Jesus speaks to and like Maisy's dad, we allow the 'deaths', both literal and figurative, to consume us?

God IS. Not WAS. Through everything, good and bad, happy and sad. Through little disappointments, through the many losses involved in just living our lives, and most of all through what we call 'death', **God steadily and persistently offers 'LIVE POWER!', resurrection power!**

So each time you experience disappointment, each time you go through those 'little deaths' involved in life here on earth, remember that God is always present to bring you new life.
Always.

Reflections

How <u>do</u> we get so hung up in the details that they consume our focus and become the reason we live each day?

Name some ways that we allow the 'deaths', both literal and figurative, to consume us:

As individuals:

As households?

As a nation?

As a world?

How would you describe Maisy's "LIVE POWER!" active in the world and/or in our lives?

32

Life's Love Anchor

When the Pharisees heard that he had silenced the Sadducees, they gathered together, and one of them, a lawyer, asked him a question to test him. "Teacher, which commandment in the law is the greatest?"

He said to him, "'You shall love the Lord your God with all your heart, and with all your soul, and with all your mind.' This is the greatest and first commandment. And a second is like it: 'You shall love your neighbor as yourself.' On these two commandments hang all the law and the prophets."

Now while the Pharisees were gathered together, Jesus asked them this question: "What do you think of the Messiah? Whose son is he?" They said to him, "The son of David."

He said to them, "How is it then that David by the Spirit calls him Lord, saying, 'The Lord said to my Lord, "Sit at my right hand, until I put your enemies under your feet" '? If David thus calls him Lord, how can he be his son?"

No one was able to give him an answer, nor from that day did anyone dare to ask him any more questions.
- *Matthew 22: 34-46 (New Revised Standard Version)*

When the crowds heard him, they were impressed with his teaching. But when the Pharisees heard that he had silenced the Sadducees with his reply, they thought up a fresh question of their own to ask him.

One of them, an expert in religious law, tried to trap him with this question: "Teacher, which is the most important commandment in the law of Moses?"

Jesus replied, "'You must love the Lord your God with all your heart, all your soul, and all your mind.' This is the first and greatest commandment. A second is equally important: 'Love your neighbor as yourself.' All the other commandments and all the demands of the prophets are based on these two commandments."

Then, surrounded by the Pharisees, Jesus asked them a question: "What do you think about the Messiah? Whose son is he?" They replied, "He is the son of David."

Jesus responded, "Then why does David, speaking under the inspiration of the Holy Spirit, call him Lord? For David said, 'The LORD said to my Lord, Sit in honor at my right hand until I humble your enemies beneath your feet.' Since David called him Lord, how can he be his son at the same time?"

No one could answer him. And after that, no one dared to ask him any more questions.
- *Matthew 22: 34-46 (New Living Translation)*

* * * * * * * * * *

Sharon and Jack had adopted children because they'd both been told they couldn't have any. So now that they were happy (and very busy) parents of **three 'special needs' children,** Sharon found out she was– **surprise! –pregnant.** Not just pregnant, but as her husband Jack put it, "REALLY pregnant". At three months, Sharon looked more like she was five (or more) months along. **So here they were getting their first sonogram.**

Seven year old Max, their oldest, was being entertained in the waiting room by one of the office assistants while Sharon and Jack were busy with the test. A **bubbly boy with an infectious grin,** Jack was busily creating a picture at the kids' art table. His Down's syndrome had given Max a **very small (five word) vocabulary,** but his attention and creativity were glued to his picture. He worked and hummed, hummed and worked...

Meanwhile, **Jack and Sharon got the surprise of their lives** – not one, but THREE babies were coming! They were speechless, simply staring at the screen as the technician pointed out each little one on the screen. Before they knew it, Sharon was dressed again and they were headed back out to the waiting area with a folder full of sonogram pictures.

Max was ready. Flashing the sign for 'how many?', he added 'baby' – and waited expectantly. Jack paused. Would he understand the magnitude of the changes coming to their family? They'd only had Max a year, and he'd certainly blossomed in that time. But this, this was something else. The other two were younger – five year old Tess (who had MS) and two year old Micah (who was deaf from a head injury) had come into their family two years ago.

Jack squatted down to Max's eye level. "Well, Sport, we've got great news! Mommy's got three babies in her tummy!" He paused, examining Max's young face to see if he understood, and trying to figure out what he might be thinking about it.

Max paused a moment, then ran over to the kids' art table to get his drawing. Looking up into Jack's face, Max struggled to express what he wanted to say. He stammered, **"pppppresenttt!"** and handed his creation to Jack. It was a drawing of **a beautiful anchor with heart stickers all over it and the word 'Love' written right on the anchor.**

The office assistant came over to explain. "You were in there a long time, and Max got really worried. I told him I could tell what a wonderful son he was, and what a big help he must be to you. **He wanted you to know about this anchor of love.** I think when he was worried, he knew that whatever was wrong, love would get you all through. I read a book with him about love, and he copied 'love' right from the cover onto his drawing for you."

Sharon spoke up. **"Max surprises us all the time.** We were a little worried about all the responsibility of adopting him, but how can you resist that smile? Anyway, we overheard his social worker telling Max how it would be so wonderful with us – because our family was anchored in love. I guess that's stuck with him this whole time!"

Life's love anchor. Jack and Sharon hung everything on that anchor. Learning sign language. Dealing with leg braces and wheelchairs and walkers. Figuring out how to communicate with Max and help him be all he could be. And now, **well now there's just going to be more love anchoring to do.** And a lot of planning, oh yes, a lot of changes coming!

* * * * * * * * *

Pharisees. Saduccees. Zealots. Essenes. Just a few of the 'denominations' of Jesus' day. All of them were trying to figure out what was most important. Out of the 613+ Laws, which were the 'have to's'? the 'shoulds'? the 'really ought to's'. **Like many denominations today, each had their own opinions.** The Saduccees had just been silenced, stumped by this Teacher Jesus, this powerful Prophet, whom many were claiming was the Messiah. Now it was the Pharisees' turn to try. **Whose denominational camp would Jesus fit into?**

Seeking to make Him 'fit', they questioned Him, thinking to trap him into giving his denominational allegiance away. **I wonder what they hoped his answer would be?**

His answer stunned them (and probably irritated them too, since it was straight out of the most basic part of the holy Torah!). Jesus pointed them directly to what is called the 'Sh'ma', the fundamental statement of the Law's grounding: Love God with all you are and love your neighbor as yourself. **Love. Yep, that's it, Jesus told them: LOVE!**

I can just **picture the same scene today,** can't you? Imagine representatives from any of the many denominations (or even a 'nondenominational' church). Can you see them questioning Jesus? I **think the result would be pretty much the same. Love would be the Word.**
Hear Him again:

Jesus replied, " 'You must love the Lord your God with all your heart, all your soul, and all your mind.' This is the first and greatest commandment. A second is equally important: 'Love your neighbor as yourself.' All the other commandments and all the demands of the prophets are based on these two commandments."

How would today's church representatives handle Jesus' follow up question? It's essentially asking what authority Jesus has for them. In other words, what authority does Jesus' answer carry? Where does it fit into their priorities for living?

They asked – what's the most important law to live by?
Jesus told them to anchor their lives in love. Sounds simple, doesn't it?

So **here we are, a couple thousand years later.** Same story, same questions, same answer.

Are our whole lives anchored the way Jesus tells us? (No, but we're trying....)
How hard are we trying? (well....)

Sounds like a good spiritual project!
So....What anchors your life?
Is your life anchored in God's love, love for God, love for your neighbors?

Check your life's anchor each day, and may it be more and more filled with God's incredible.....LOVE!

Reflections

How do you think today's church representatives wouldhandle Jesus' follow up question?

What do you think is the most important law to live by?

33

Jus' Walkin'

Then Jesus said to the crowds and to his disciples,"The teachers of religious law and the Pharisees are the official interpreters of the Scriptures. So practice and obey whatever they say to you, **but don't follow their example.**

For they don't practice what they teach. They crush you with impossible religious demands and never lift a finger to help ease the burden.

Everything they do is for show. On their arms they wear extra wide prayer boxes with Scripture verses inside, and they wear extra long tassels on their robes.And how they love to sit at the head table at banquets and in the most prominent seats in the synagogue!They enjoy the attention they get on the streets, and they enjoy being called 'Rabbi.'

Don't ever let anyone call you 'Rabbi,' for you have only one teacher, and all of you are on the same level as brothers and sisters. And don't address anyone here on earth as 'Father,' for only God in heaven is your spiritual Father.And don't let anyone call you 'Master,' for there is only one master, the Messiah.

The greatest among you must be a servant. But those who exalt themselves will be humbled, and those who humble themselves will be exalted. - Matthew 23: 1-12 (New Living Translation)

Now Jesus turned to address his disciples, along with the crowd that had gathered with them. "The religion scholars and Pharisees are competent teachers in God's Law. You won't go wrong in following their teachings on Moses. But **be careful about following THEM.**

They talk a good line, but they don't live it. They don't take it into their hearts and live it out in their behavior. It's all spit-and-polish veneer.

"Instead of giving you God's Law as food and drink by which you can banquet on God, they package it in bundles of rules, loading you down like pack animals. They seem to take pleasure in watching you stagger under these loads, and wouldn't think of lifting a finger to help.

Their lives are perpetual fashion shows, embroidered prayer shawls one day and flowery prayers the next. They love to sit at the head table at church dinners, basking in the most prominent positions, preening in the radiance of public flattery, receiving honorary degrees, and getting called 'Doctor' and 'Reverend'.

"Don't let people do that to YOU, put you on a pedestal like that. You all have a single Teacher, and you are all classmates. Don't set people up as experts over your life, letting them tell you what to do. Save that authority for God; let HIM tell you what to do. No one else should carry the title of 'Father'; you have only one Father, and he's in heaven. And don't let people maneuver you into taking charge of them. **There is only one Life-Leader for you and them – Christ.**

"Do you want to stand out? Then step down. Be a servant. If you puff yourself up, you'll get the wind knocked out of you. **But if you're content to simply be yourself, your life will count for plenty."**

- Matthew 23: 1-12 (The Message Version)

* * * * * * * * *

Jus' Walkin'. For the longest time, I thought that had to be his name. Well, or maybe a nickname of some sort. I ran across him the first time I visited the 'projects' (officially called 'welfare apartments') in downtown St. Louis.

"Jus' walkin'" was his answer to everything, it seemed.
"Hey, how're you doing?"
"Jus' walkin'."

One day I tried something different. "Good morning. Nice day. You out enjoying this fine spring sunshine?"
His answer – you guessed it – was....
"Jus' walkin'."

Now **I was new in the neighborhood,** so I asked an elderly lady I'd become acquainted with about him. **"Oh,"** she smiled at me, **"Him? He's Jus' Walkin'"**

"No ma'am," I answered, sure she'd misunderstood my question, **"I mean to ask, what's his name?"**

"Well, preacher girl, I reckon that's it – Jus' Walkin'."
She paused, somehow knowing me to be the curious type. Her smile got bigger until it became a fun-loving giggle. **"Girl, you just watch him sometime.** Watch what he does. Don't be worryin' none about what he do – or don't – say. Just be watchin. You have a nice day now." And she stepped inside her little apartment and shut the door, still smiling and shaking her head.

So I followed her advice. I worked hard to notice what 'Jus' Walkin' was doing. What I learned about him was simply amazing. **He walked a lot alright:** back and forth to the drug store to pick up prescriptions for homebound folks in the projects apartments. He took a little boy in a wheelchair for long neighborhood walks. He delivered blankets and sandwiches to the homeless folks who squatted behind the apartments at night. He walked a scared runaway teenage girl to the police station so she could get a ride home. The list went on.

Weeks went by, and **my amazement at his ministry grew.** One day I was asked to give a new minister in town a tour of that neighborhood. Sure enough, one of the first people we met was Jus' Walkin'. After I introduced the two men, and we'd moved on down the street, my companion remarked, **"Wow, now HE looks weird. And he doesn't even know his own name. Are there a lot like him down here?"**

Now it was me smiling, me trying hard (unsuccessfully I might add) to suppress a giggle as I replied. "No, my friend, you won't meet too many like him. Not 'down here', not anywhere really. Nope, **Jus' Walkin' is one of a kind. I think he's a walking Bible really. Wait till you notice – really notice – what he does. That'll tell you who he really is."**

* * * * * * * * *

I wonder how it would be if <u>our</u> vocabulary was suddenly limited to 2 words. What would happen if others had to describe us based on what we did, how we treated each other, and what we spent our time and energy on?

If you had two words to describe yourself, what would they be? If every time you introduced yourself, you had to **claim those two words in place of your name,** could you? Would you?

Jus' Walkin' indeed took his faith into his heart and lived it. He was a living example of Jesus' life instruction: *"...step down. Be a servant.... if you're content to simply be yourself, your life will count for plenty."*

How about us?

Reflections

If you had two words to describe yourself, what would they be?

If every time you introduced yourself, you had to **claim those two words in place of your name**, could you? Would you?

How have people been "walking Bibles" in your life?

Think of some possible two word descriptions for these "walking Bibles"...what are some of them?

34

Roadblocks

"I've had it with you! You're hopeless, you religion scholars, you Pharisees! Frauds! **Your lives are roadblocks to God's kingdom. You refuse to enter, and won't let anyone else in either.**

"You're hopeless, you religion scholars and Pharisees! Frauds! You go halfway around the world to make a convert, but once you get him you make him into a replica of yourselves, double-damned.

"You're hopeless! What arrogant stupidity! You say, 'If someone makes a promise with his fingers crossed, that's nothing; but if he swears with his hand on the bible, that's serious.' What ignorance! Does the leather on the Bible carry more weight than the skin on your hands?

"And what about this piece of trivia? 'If you shake hands on a promise, that's nothing; but if you raise your hand that God is your witness, that's serious'? What ridiculous hair-splitting! What difference does it make if you shake hands or raise hands? A promise is a promise. What difference does it make if you make your promise inside or outside a house of worship? A promise is a promise. **God is present, watching and holding you to account regardless.**

"You're hopeless, you religion scholars and Pharisees! Frauds! You keep meticulous account books, tithing on every nickel and dime you get, **but on the meat of God's Law, things like fairness and compassion and commitment – the absolute basics! – you carelessly take it or leave it.** *Careful bookkeeping is commendable, but the basics are required.* **Do you have any idea how silly you look,** *writing a life story that's wrong from start to finish, nitpicking over commas and semicolons?*

"You're hopeless, you religion scholars and Pharisees! Frauds! You burnish the surface of your cups and bowls so they sparkle in the sun, while the insides are maggoty with your greed and gluttony. Stupid Pharisee! **Scour the insides, and then the gleaming surface will mean something!**

"You're hopeless, you religion scholars and Pharisees! Frauds! You're like manicured grave plots, grass-clipped and flowers bright, but six feet down it's all rotting bones and worm-eaten flesh. **People who look at you and think you're saints, but beneath the skin you're total frauds."**

- Matthew 23: 13-28 (The Message Version)

* * * * * * * * *

The first conversation was really over before it began. The line at the local coffee shop was backed up (new drink maker training) so folks began to visit while they waited. Talk turned to church as **one guy tried to talk another into 'finding Jesus so you know you're going to heaven'.**

Lots of smiles and nods – until the guy walked out the door. Then the REAL conversation began.

"I know HIM!" one man exclaimed. "Our kids play on the same team. You should have seen him at the last game. **Man! And THAT'S a Christian? Wow."**

Yet another had a similar response. **"Yeah, and he's not the nicest character in here either."** That got the attention of one of the workers, who just nodded a definite 'yes'."

"So, what I don't get is, well, **I'm not really up on this 'church stuff', but I've heard that**, well..." This from a guy who'd been quietly listening so far. Folks all turned to listen, even the one who'd just gotten his drink. "Go on," one of them encouraged him.

"Well, **my teenage son, I think he's on to something.** We were talking about just this thing on the way home from his basketball practice yesterday. It seems his coach told him something real interesting. Todd, that's my son, **he said he finally got up the nerve to ask coach what made him have such integrity** – even when it was hard, like when they lost their last game by 40 points. Want to know what his coach said?"

Now everyone was listening as he continued. "Well, **Todd said coach just smiled and told him, 'Son, sometimes, well sometimes Jesus does just fine till people get ahold of Him.** Then it can get really interesting. Yes it can, so Todd, you make real sure to find out about The Guy yourself first. Folks who mean well (and some who don't) **can really put big roadblocks in your way**, and pretty soon **you'll be on a road that, well, they may CALL it Christian, but it'll have nothing to do with Christ.'** Coach made such an impression on my boy, why we spent the whole evening talking about it!"

* * * * * * * * * *

Upon reading the above response of the coach, your response might be something like, **"Isn't that why Jesus came? Wasn't it so people could get 'ahold of' a relationship with the Living God?"** Well, yes, and therein lies the key to the whole thing. It's about relationship. Relationship is an 'inside job' as one of my friends once put it. She was fond of saying, **"It's when you show what's really inside, how you really are. It just sort of comes out."**

And what's more important than our relationship with God? More important than our discipleship relationship with Christ? Nothing. That's right, nothing is more important.

We all have roles we play in life, but it's who and what we are core-deep that comes through in every situation, every encounter, every test life throws at us that shows who, and Whose, we really are.

Do we mess up? You bet! Are we perfect? Not by a long shot! But **relationship is about commitment.** Commitment to keep trying. Commitment to stick with it. Commitment to an ever closer, deeper relationship!

That's what infuriated Jesus with these religion scholars, these Pharisees. They'd lost sight of relationship. For them, it had become all about LOOKING good, LOOKING like they were holy and close to God. Like Todd's coach said, they had become lost on a road they thought was Godly, one they thought had them close to God, but they'd lost sight of that God-relationship road long ago. **They'd become their own roadblocks to living in God's grace.** Worse than that (and I think what made Jesus speak to them this way) is the fact that they **were leading many others down the same roadblocked path.**

So, take time to 'know The Guy'. Pray. Read your Bible. Ask yourself these questions as you read and pray: Who IS this God who loves me so much? Who IS this Jesus who loved me so much he gave His life for me? Find some Christ-following friends, some who are also learning more every day about the saving grace they're discovering in Jesus. Pray together. Talk about your relationships with God, with Jesus.

All of these spiritual practices will help you spot – and avoid – just the sort of roadblocks Jesus is talking about. I pray that your own relationship with God and your own discipleship journey become deeper and richer each and every day!

Reflections

What "roadblocks" have you experienced in your own developing life of faith?

How have (or are) you overcoming them?

Why is Jesus so down on these Pharisees? I mean, surely He doesn't expect them to be perfect! What would your answer be to this statement?

35

What Tradition?

"How terrible it will be for you teachers of religious law and you Pharisees. Hypocrites! For you build tombs for the prophets your ancestors killed and decorate the graves of the godly people your ancestors destroyed.

Then **you say, 'We never would have joined them in killing the prophets.'**

"In saying that, you are accusing yourselves of being the descendants of those who murdered the prophets. Go ahead. Finish what they started. Snakes! Sons of vipers! How will you escape the judgment of hell?

I will send you prophets and wise men and teachers of religious law. You will kill some by crucifixion and whip others in your synagogues, chasing them from city to city. As a result, you will become guilty of murdering all the godly people from righteous Abel to Zechariah son of Barachiah, whom you murdered in the Temple between the altar and the sanctuary. I assure you, all the accumulated judgment of the centuries will break upon the heads of this very generation.

"O Jerusalem, Jerusalem, the city that kills the prophets and stones God's messengers! How often I have wanted to gather your children together as a hen protects her chicks beneath her wings, but you wouldn't let me. And now look, your house is left to you, empty and desolate. For I tell you this, you will never see me again until you say, 'Bless the one who comes in the name of the Lord!' "

- Matthew 23: 29-39 (New Living Translation)

* * * * * * * * * *

He arrived early for the job interview. *Wow, were there ever **a lot of people** waiting! I wonder what my chances are of getting this job?* Brian thought about this and more as he sat pretending to read the magazine and 'scoped out' what he thought might be his job competition. *They all look so different. Younger. Older. Suit-and-tie. Slacks and polo. Very interesting.* He hoped he'd made the right choice – khakis, shirt, and tie.

Just then two doors opened and two names were called out (not his – rats!). **He kept waiting.** Four more people arrived, got magazines, and sat down. The curious look on his face must have given him away. The woman next to him smiled. **"Hey, I'm Jackie. Which position are you applying for?"** *Which position? OK, don't act stupid.* "I'm interviewing for the accounts payable position. And you?"

She smiled again. "I'm hoping for the CFO spot. My dream job. Makes me a little nervous, though. Know what I'm talking about?" Brian had no clue what she was talking about, and she seemed to know it, so she added, "I'm sorry. **I bet you think these folks are all here for the same opening, huh?"**

Now he really felt unprepared. He'd researched the company and felt ready to apply, but....

"Yeah, they have **ten openings to fill. Real nasty scandal.** They're trying to get past it, you know, fix their reputation. I almost decided not to apply, but something about turning it around really attracted me. Hey, you OK?"

Brian felt OK – caught a little off guard, but OK. Good thing he found out about this now! **"Thanks, Jackie. I think you just kept me from looking really stupid in there – if I ever get in there!"**

Scandal. Scandal......should I ask? Be good to know what I'm getting into – maybe...

"So Jackie, what did they do, I mean TEN openings? Must have really been something!"

She took a breath. A big one. He could tell she was wondering if she should have said anything in the first place. "Well, **think bribery, extortion, and fraud.** What a thing to get out of, huh? I know the guy who blew the whistle too. He's somewhere far away now. New name, new job, new everything. The government's helping him out. What intrigued me was what the CEO said about the whole thing. I met him at a big event out east a couple of months ago. Know what he told me?"

Brian was still stunned. *Bribery, extortion, fraud? How did you outlive THAT?* Maybe he should get out of here now... He started to get up, but Jackie's next words stopped him.

"Well, Mr. Jacobs looked me right in the eye. Then he said**...**"**We need a new tradition.** We've got a record. **We know what people expect**, and we intend to surprise them. I'm building a solid base – a rock solid, arrow straight, do-it-right-or-else.....tradition."

"So Jackie, **how many people did he keep?** I mean, how many agreed, and were worthy to stay?"

"Four."

"Four? Out of how many here in the main office?"

Doors opened again. Names were called, not theirs. Brian's mind spun. Four left....

"Twenty-five, Brian. There were twenty-five."

Just then, another door opened. **"Jackie Myer? Brian Johns? This way please."**

Together? It was then he realized that **everyone was being called in pairs.**

As they entered the office, **a smiling man addressed Jackie.** "Well, what do you think?" Brian's mouth almost fell open as he realized – that whole conversation with Jackie had been an interview! **"Well,"** Jackie replied, a **sparkle in her eye, "I think he'll be good to work with.** How about it, Mr. Brian Johns, think you could work here? Ready to create something new from the ashes of an awful reputation and a bad track record? **Ready for a new...TRADITION?"**

Still in shock, Brian scrambled to regain his normally logical thinking (not quite successfully). **"You're.... you're... the CEO! You're Mr. Jacobs!"**

"Yep. That would be me. **Are you ready to break the record and make the tradition?"**

And **that's how Brian Johns got his big break.** That companydefied expectations. They <u>demolished</u> the old reputation, the old record. **Within five years, the company quadrupled its business.** Very few outsiders even <u>connected</u> the old corrupt company with the new one.

Beyond all expectations, beyond their bad reputation, they'd built a rock-solid, straight tradition of integrity.

*   *   *   *   *   *   *   *   *   *

Ever done anything you're not proud of? Most of us (OK, all of us probably) have.
Ever get another chance? Most of us have (whether we recognize it or not).

Seems once you've messed up, made wrong choices, two things happen. First, the more of those wrong choices you make, the easier, the more 'natural' they get. Second, others begin to expect us to behave 'the way we always have' in their eyes.

*Jesus: "For I tell you this, **you will never see me again until you say, 'Bless the one who comes in the name of the Lord!'**"*

Jesus challenges and calls us through this Scripture to live and behave in ways that demonstrate that WE indeed bless 'the One who comes in the name of the Lord (Jesus)'. He also challenges us to recognize others who (though imperfect) live in ways that show they know and recognize Jesus every day.

It's the Jesus-tradition!

How about it? Most of us have spent days (or weeks, or....) far from this 'Jesus-tradition'.
The incredible Good News is that it's never too late to come back. Listen to the words of Hebrews 12:1-2:

*"Therefore, since **we are surrounded by so great a cloud of witnesses, let us also lay aside every weight and the sin that clings so closely, and let us run with perseverance the race that is set before us, looking to Jesus the pioneer and perfecter of our faith,** who for the sake of the joy that was set before Him endured the cross, disregarding its shame, and has taken His seat at the right hand of the throne of God."* (New Living Translation)

Wow! There's a whole crowd rooting for you! So when you wonder where you're headed, what's your pattern for life (your "tradition"), how about this response:

What tradition? Why, I'm in the.....Jesus tradition!!

Reflections

What do you think of the statement:

"Seems once you've messed up, made wrong choices, two things happen. First, the more of those wrong choices you make, the easier, the more 'natural' they get. Second, others begin to expect us to behave 'the way we always have' in their eyes."?

How does that play out in real life?

How do you think Jesus was setting a "new tradition"?

How do you see that playing out in today's world?

36

This is GOOD News?

As Jesus was leaving the Temple grounds, his disciples pointed out to him the various Temple buildings. But he told them, **"Do you see all these buildings? I assure you, they will be so completely demolished that not one stone will be left on top of another!"**

Later, Jesus sat on the slopes of the Mount of Olives. His disciples came to him privately and asked, **"When will all this take place? And will there be any sign ahead of time** *to signal your return and the end of the world?"*

Jesus told them, **"Don't let anyone mislead you.** *For many will come in my name, saying, 'I am the Messiah.' They will lead many astray. And wars will break out near and far, but* **don't panic.** *Yes,* **these things must come, but the end won't follow immediately.** *The nations and kingdoms will proclaim war against each other, and there will be* **famines and earthquakes** *in many parts of the world. But all this will be* **only the beginning of the horrors to come.**

"Then you will be **arrested, persecuted, and killed.** *You will be* **hated** *all over the world because of your allegiance to me. And many will turn away from me and betray and hate each other. And many false prophets will appear and will lead many people astray. Sin will be rampant everywhere, and the* **love of many will grow cold.**

"But those who endure to the end will be saved. And the Good News about the Kingdom will be preached throughout the whole world, so that all nations will hear it; and then, finally, the end will come."

– Matthew 24: 1-14 (New Living Translation)

* * * * * * * * * *

"She's right over there, Chaplain. Said she'd wait however long it took you to get here. Her name's Maureen. You know, in all the months she's been coming here, **I've never seen her so excited! Don't know about what, because, well, the chemo's not working,** but, well,...there she is – over there." With that, the nurse pointed out a very frail young woman with a beautiful silk scarf on her head and a bright smile on her face.

"Are you the chaplain?" Hopeful eyes met mine. I nodded and took a seat next to her. "Well, I'm **Maureen,"** she said, **"and I've finally figured it out – I got it!"** I know my puzzlement was clear as day, because she smiled again, **opened the Bible she held on her lap**, and pointed at the page. I got my Bible out of my briefcase and opened it too. Interesting selection. **Not at all what I expected her to turn to.**

Her eyes twinkled. "Bet you're wondering why I picked such a horrible-sounding thing, aren't you? Well, let me tell you, **I always avoided these sorts of Bible readings before** – just skipped right over them to the next happy verses, you know?"

"**But then I realized... this is just like my life with cancer!** Listen." She was really excited now! "You know, I think of all those buildings that fell apart, all those stones, they're like the pieces of my life – my job, my hobbies, things I liked to do...before this cancer came anyway. It's like they made up my life, and if we're supposed to be living temples for God, well, it makes sense, see?"

I thought I was catching on, maybe.....

"And you know what I just HAD to know in the beginningof all this, don't you? **I had to know all the signs too, just like those disciples!** 'How will I know when it's the end?' That was my favorite question! And **in spite of Jesus' 'don't panic', I sure did, more than once."**

"**I met those 'false prophets' too** – people with all those miracle cures for my cancer. Yeah, right, uh huh. Famines –**chemo'll make a good famine sound realgood, and cancer shakes your world like aRichter scale9 earthquake!"**

I was beginning to make the connection now. I'd never thought of it quite this way before. Honestly, I hadn't read these Scriptures too often either!

"**Then came the worst**," Maureen looked me straight in the eye. "Lots of my friends, even some of my family, couldn't see **how I could stay a Christ-follower through all this**. 'How could God let this happen?' they'd say, or, 'Just figure out what sin's in your life and get rid of it. The cancer will go then too!'. Oh, man. **Talk about love going cold."**

"**Cancer has arrested me, persecuted me, but you know what? It can't <u>really</u> kill me.** Oh it'll kill my body all right, but don't you see? It's just like that temple building. The real me, well, God will save that. And <u>that's</u> the GoodNews! I realized that **I'm a part of what He's talking about when He says the 'ends of the earth'** – like those far away from knowing Christ, right? Well, I've sure been there!"

I knew there was a punch line coming. I could feel it. My mind was still reeling from this new way of seeingthe Scripture she talked about, and I was unprepared for what she said next.

"Chaplain, **I've met lots of people living at the 'ends of the earth'** in their spirits, know what I mean? Well,they tell me I've only got a few weeks left here, so I've got to pass this message on. **Will you help me?** Please?"

* * * * * * * * *

I've never looked at that Scripture the same way again. Maureen ministered to me as much (or maybe more) than I ministered to her that day. I looked back at my life, and I could see what she called 'spiritual ends of the earth' inmy own past. My eyes filled with tears as I realized how God had sent people and situations into my life to bring me back, to show me grace. **I discovered the Good News of Christ all over again that day** in deeper and richer ways than ever before.

Many times when our lives are in those rough, maybe even horrible places, we shut down. We close ourselves off. We can't see <u>any</u> Good News! We fail to see the grace, the sure and steady presence of God constantly seeking us out, always ready to strengthen us – even when we're at the 'ends of the earth'.

Maybe you're at the 'ends of the earth' right now. If so, know that God will never, ever abandon you. The life, ministry, death, and most of all the resurrection of Christ prove that. Yes, THIS is Good News!

Perhaps life is pretty good for you right now. If that's you, look around. Someone you know (or maybe somebody you're about to meet) needs you to point the way back from their 'end of the earth', to show them God's unfailing grace and care, to BE the Good News – with skin on! What's stopping you? Pray about it – pray to be open to God's leading in your life.

Reflections

Where is your life right now? Rough? End-of-the-earth? Pretty good? How do you see God's "Good News" in the middle of your life?

Why do people avoid "those places" in the Bible?

37

Life's Vultures

"Someday you will see that "Horrible Thing" in the holy place, just as the prophet Daniel said. Everyone who reads this must try to understand! If you are living in Judea at that time, run to the mountains. If you are on the roof of your house, **don't go inside to get anything.** If you are out in the field, **don't go back for your coat.** It will be a **terrible time for women who are expecting babies or nursing young children.** And pray that you won't have to escape in winter or on a Sabbath. This will be the worst time of suffering since the beginning of the world, and nothing this terrible will ever happen again. If God doesn't make the time shorter, no one will be left alive. **But because of God's chosen ones, he will make the time shorter.**

"Someone may say, 'Here is the Messiah!' or 'There he is!' But don't believe it. **False messiahs and false prophets will come** and work great miracles and signs. They will even try to fool God's chosen ones. **But I have warned you ahead of time.** If you are told that the Messiah is out in the desert, don't go there! And if you are told that he is in some secret place, don't believe it!

*"**The coming of the Son of Man will be like lightning that can be seen from east to west.** Where there is a corpse, there will always be buzzards.

- Matthew 24: 15-28 (Contemporary English Version)

* * * * * * * * * *

"I think the 'Horrible Thing' is already here."

What?

"Yeah, I mean, and He's right when He says that '...nothing this terrible should ever happen again'."

Eric, a high school senior, was the president of the church youth group. **His dad was on the church leadership team. Lately it seemed no one could agree on anything.** Dates for vacation Bible school. What day of the week the church should be cleaned. What color to paint the new mailbox outside. The list went on and on. Eric knew the whole thing, said it had become at least half of their family nightly dinner table conversation.

"You know, **mom and dad talked about maybe checking out other churches.** But you know what? The churches a lot of my friends go to are the same way. I've been praying, I mean really praying for God to show me what's going on here. **Maybe we could be some of those 'chosen ones', you think?"**

Some of the other youth caught right on, but I must have looked puzzled, because Eric continued. **"OK, let's say I'm a new dad, and I'm looking for a church** – like I've got a kid now and all that. Do I really want to get involved if all they do is argue about stuff like painting the mail box and cleaning days? Is that what following Christ is all about? That connects with Jesus saying *'It will be a terrible time for women who are expecting babies or nursing young children.'* Not just moms, but anyone trying to learn what this Christianity's all about."

"Know what else? The other day I got out to the parking lot and I realized I'd left my jacket in the church, so I went back to get it. I never got there. I just decided to leave it there and get it later. Know why? As soon as I stepped into the hall I could hear people arguing, really arguing – in the sanctuary! Yelling almost, and it was all about when to have vacation Bible school!"

Eric's observations began a wonderful sharing and brainstorming time, the results of which were presented to that same leadership team. We spent almost two hours (fueled by a pizza delivery) realizing that we had a choice. We could be some of those 'chosen ones' Jesus talked about! God has indeed, 'warned us ahead of time' (lots of times, in fact). How could we be more Christ-like? How could we be God's instruments of grace in this part of the Body of Christ?

When Christ returns, *'like lightning that can be seen from east to west'*, will we be ready? That was Eric's ending question.

The youth group asked, and received, time at the beginning of the next church leadership team meeting. They **truly served up a buffet-sized portion of God's grace that day.** They were God's 'chosen ones' that day (and in many days to come). Two of the young ladies wrote a skit based on their observations and the group presented it as the Sunday message.

The church moved through shock, listening, and honest appraisal. Changes came slowly, but like a downhill roller coaster slide, **God's light and grace flowed** through that congregation again. The mailbox was painted – rainbow colors. The cleaning day – well, it really didn't matter that much. And those vacation Bible school dates? They put all the possibilities in a hat and drew one out – done!

The major change? They prayed together before making decisions. They prayed for those they disagreed with. They asked for prayers when they felt, in one's words, 'cranky'.

Amazing things happened. Guests felt it – a Godly, prayerful atmosphere. One guest said it well. **"I can just breathe in grace here.** I can feel God all over this place!" She went on to share (sadly) that she'd visited at least five other churches and almost gave up completely. Ours wasthe last chance she was giving 'church'. **She stayed – and joyfully became the one who....cleaned the church.**

Reflections

How is Eric speaking to you? How's the 'grace-meter' in your life? Your family? Your work or school environment? Your friendship group?

God chooses us – chooses a relationship with us. How do we choose God? Are we part of God's 'Chosen Ones' or do we look more like part of the 'Horrible Thing'?

What are we going to do about it?

38

Are We THERE Yet?

"Immediately after the suffering of those days the sun will be darkened, and the moon will not give its light; the stars will fall from heaven, and the powers of heaven will be shaken.

"Then the sign of the Son of Man will appear in heaven, and then all the tribes of the earth will mourn, and they will see 'the Son of Man coming on the clouds of heaven' with power and great glory. And he will send out his angels with a loud trumpet call, and they will gather his elect from the four winds, from one end of heaven to the other.

"From the fig tree learn its lesson: as soon as its branch becomes tender and puts forth its leaves, you know that summer is near. So also, when you see all these things, you know that he is near, at the very gates. *Truly I tell you, this generation will not pass away until all these things have taken place.* ***Heaven and earth will pass away, but my words will not pass away.***

- Matthew 24: 29-35 (New Revised Standard Version)

"Following those hard times, Sun will fade out, moon cloud over, stars fall out of the sky, cosmic powers tremble.

" Then, the Arrival of the Son of man! It will fill the skies – no one will miss it. Unready people all over the world, outsiders to the splendor and power, will raise a huge lament as they watch the Son of Man blazing out of heaven. At that same moment, he'll dispatch his angels with a trumpet-blast summons, pulling in God's chosen from the four winds, from pole to pole.

"Take a lesson from the fig tree. From the moment you notice its buds form, the merest hint of green, you know summer's just around the corner. So it is with you: When you see all these things, you'll know he's at the door. Don't take this lightly. I'm not just saying this for some future generation, but for all of you. This age continues until all these things take place. Sky and earth will wear out; my words won't wear out.

– Matthew 24: 29-35 (The Message Version)

* * * * * * * * * *

The **family van fairly bubbled with excitement.** The closer they got to grandma and grandpa's farm, the more frequently **'Are we there YET?'** popped up from the kids.

"Kids, remember about the stuff I told you we'd pass on the way?", dad reminded them, getting really tired of the 'are we there yet' refrains ringing in his ears.

"Yep dad, I got the list right here." Trust his fifteen year old, detail-oriented son to be prepared for just such a question!

"OK, let's see..." fifteen year old Brad pulled out his notebook. "Hmmm. Let's see. McDonald's over the highway, check. Kansas City, check. Big herd of cow statues on the side of the road, check. Nothing for miles, check – just kidding Dad, just kidding!" Father and son laughed together.

"So Brad, what's left on the list?" Mom asked, turning around from the front seat. She'd been down this road to her hometown and the farm so many times she no longer even noticed the landmarks and interesting things on the way.

So they went down the list of what to look for on the rest of the trip, deciding to make a game of who noticed things first.

"I can't wait to go fishing!" Alicia, at six years old the youngest of the five kids, piped up.
"I want to pet a cow!", eight year old Ben called out.
Not to be outdone, eleven year old Kate leaned forward and whispered in mom's ear, "And I want to take care of all those cats grandma has!"

Soon they were down to the lastitem on Brad's 'going to the farm' list. "There it is – the purple barn!" the excited chorus rose from the kids as they turned down the road leading to their grandparents' house. This would be an awesome summer!

* * * * * * * * * *

So how do you know you're on the right path in your life, the path moving you closer and closer in your relationship with God, your walk as Jesus' follower? Are there signs, 'stuff on the way' you can identify?

Jesus is knocking continually on the door of our lives. Revelation 3:20 says, *"Listen! I am standing at the door, knocking; if you hear my voice and open the door, I will come in to you and eat with you, and you with me." (New Living Translation)*

So, ARE we 'there yet'? No. Here's a better question: Are we getting there? Do we see signs in our own lives that we're getting closer and closer? There are three possible answers:

YES. Great! Keep on traveling! Keep seeking and following God's will for you as Christ's disciple, knowing that when you make mistakes, you just need to get 'back on track'.

NO. Well, reread that Scripture above from Revelation 3:20. Open your heart's door, your mind'sdoor, your life's door – to Christ. Pray. Take time (even a little – it'll grow on you as the Holy Spirit lights your life. He's right there, a breath away, just waiting for you to let Him in!

I HAVE NO IDEA. This is an honest answer that more folks than you know would respond with if they're really being honest. Life can get so busy, so hectic, and so bogged down that you truly have no idea where you are on your faith journey. Begin by thinking about your day. Try to identify the ways God touched you today, through situations and people you've encountered. If you make this a habit at the end of each day, soon you'll notice God at work in your life as it happens. Before you know it, you'll not only know where you are in your faith journey, but the path before you will clear up too!

Are 'fig trees blooming' in your life? Probably. Have you noticed them? Maybe not.

"So it is with you: When you see all these things, you'll know he's at the door. Don't take this lightly. I'm not just saying this for some future generation, <u>but for all of you</u>."

May you see and experience Christ at your door and in your life each and every day.
He's not just here for someone else, but for each of us – for YOU!! Let Him in.

Reflections

So are you "there yet"? Are you getting there?

Which fits you right now: YES? NO? I HAVE NO IDEA?

What are some things you think would be on a "check list" for a life journey growing closer to God?

39

Who Knows? Who Cares?

*"However, **no one knows the day or the hour when these things will happen, not even the angels in heaven or the Son himself.** Only the Father knows.*

*"When the Son of Man returns, it will be like it was in Noah's day. In those days before the Flood, the people were enjoying banquets and parties and weddings right up to the time Noah entered his boat. **People didn't realize what was going to happen** until the Flood came and swept them all away.*

*"**That is the way it will be when the Son of Man comes.** Two men will be working together in the field; one will be taken, the other left. Two women will be grinding flour at the mill; one will be taken, the other left. **So be prepared, because you don't know what day your Lord is coming.***

*"Know this: A homeowner who knew exactly when a burglar was coming would stay alert and not permit the house to be broken into. You also must **be ready all the time. For the Son of Man will come when least expected.***

*"Who is a faithful, sensible servant, to whom the master can give the responsibility of managing his household and feeding his family? If the master returns and finds that the servant has done a good job, there will be a reward. I assure you, the master will put that servant in charge of all he owns. But if the servant is evil and thinks, 'My master won't be back for a while,' and begins oppressing the other servants, partying, and getting drunk – well, the **master will return unannounced and unexpected.** He will tear the servant apart and banish him with the hypocrites. In that place there will be weeping and gnashing of teeth.*

- Matthew 24: 36-51 (New Living Translation)

* * * * * * * * * *

"It's not fair! You told us you weren't coming home till at least 10 o'clock!" *The pitch of the whine increased to the level of fingernails on a chalkboard as Mindy's* eyes met her dad's across the living room – a living room littered with pizza boxes, soda (and beer) cans....and four kids who weren't supposed to be there.

Dad's voice was serious (when he found it). "We need to talk. And your friends need to go. Now." *Ten seconds (if that) later, Mindy and her dad stood face to face across the trashed living room.* "So," he began, **"This whole mess is my fault because I came home early – is that about it?"**

Mindy hesitated (but not long enough for her good sense to kick in). **"But da-a-a-d! We would have had all this cleaned up if you'd just come home when you said you were going to – really!"**

"Mmmm hmmm..." was all Dad could manage immediately. He looked around. "Pizza, OK. Soda, OK. Four friends here when they're not supposed to be, not good. Beer, well, we both know that five kids all under 16.... worse than bad. So, what do you suggest now? And I'd say we'd better **get this figured out before Mom gets here in about, oh, five minutes.** She called me from the airport. All she wants to do is put her feet up and watch a movie – in the nice clean living room, by the way."

* * * * * * * * * *

OK, let's be honest here. Many of us live our lives exactly this way.

"Oh, I know I'm missing something big. I'm not really, you know, connected with God, but really, I'm busy now. **I'll take care of that later.**" This was the last thing a woman said to her best friend – before she died in an accident.

"Jesus? Yeah, I know who He is. Learned about that when I was a kid. **I'm retiring next year. Then I'll have time for that kind of thing.**" – from a conversation with a middle aged man on an airplane.

"Officer, can I call a pastor? My parents'll be so mad. What's the pastor's name? Well, it's Reverend...... somebody. Anyway, it's that church down the street – you know the one, right? Well, I guess I haven't been there in a while. Didn't really need it...well...I guess I thought I didn't...." - young man to a police officer at his roadside arrest for DUI.

<u>Which is your favorite</u>?

Later. (putting God on hold)

Some other time. (I'll be back, God, when I don't have anything else, anything more important to do)

When I REALLY need God. (don't call me, God; I'll call you!)

* * * * * * * * * *

So, who knows? You should, and God does.

Who cares? You should, and God definitely does!

What's littering your life, crowding God out of YOUR 'living room'? Like Mindy, most of us have trash (like her empty pizza boxes), temptations and sin (like those beer cans), and unhealthy influences that we choose to give space in our lives (like those friendsthey allknew weren't supposed to be there).

If you were to die unexpectedly today, what's the first thing you'd say to Jesus when you met Him?

Planning to 'retire to religion'? You're missing all the blessings, strength, and joy of a living relationship with God – you could have itTODAY!

Figure you'll call God when you need Him? You do know God's already there before you arrive, don't you? How will you recognize Him?

Remember, **God knows** all about you – and loves you deeply anyway.

Remember, **God cares** – so deeply He sent Jesus to give His all – to show us just how much.

It's true, no one knows when Jesus will return. No one knows when the 'end of the age' will come. No one except God.

But come what may, God WILL recognize those who have a living relationship with Him. Will God say to you, *"Well done, good and faithful servant!"*? *(Matthew 25: 21-23, New Living Translation)*

Don't wait!
Begin and grow your faith life, your relationship with our Living God – TODAY.
God is ready and waiting for you... *"Ask, and it will be given you; search, and you will find; knock, and the door will be opened for you. For everyone who asks receives, and everyone who searches finds, and for everyone who knocks, the door will be opened."* *(Matthew 7: 7-8)*

Reflections

Which is <u>your</u> favorite (Later? Some other time? When I REALLY need God?)? Why?

What's littering the "living room" of your life?

40

Travelin' Light

"The Kingdom of Heaven can be illustrated by the story of ten bridesmaids who took their lamps and went to meet the bridegroom. Five of them were foolish, and five were wise.

"The five who were foolish took no oil for their lamps, but the other five were wise enough to take along extra oil.

*"When the **bridegroom was delayed,** they all lay down and slept.*

"At midnight they were roused by the shout, 'Look, the bridegroom is coming! Come out and welcome him!' All the bridesmaids got up and prepared their lamps.

*"**Then the five foolish ones asked the others, 'Please give us some of your oil** because our lamps are going out.' But the others replied, 'We don't have enough for all of us. **Go to a shop and buy some for yourselves.'** "But while they were gone to buy oil, the bridegroom came, and those who were ready went in with him to the marriage feast, and **the door was locked.***

"Later, when the other five bridesmaids returned, they stood outside, calling, 'Sir, open the door for us!' But he called back, 'I don't know you!'

*"**So stay awake and be prepared, because you do not know the day or hour of my return."***

- Matthew 25: 1-13 (New Living Translation)

* * * * * * * * * *

"Come ON! No one'll know. I just didn't have time to study. I'm runnin' on empty here; can't you help me this once? Just hold up one finger for 'a', two for 'b', just like this."

Bob was horrified. His best friend Ted had never asked him to do anything like THIS. **"Hey, buddy, I just can't do that.** You're going to have to figure it out yourself. Sorry."

So Ted sweated it out. He just HAD to pass this test. If his grades dropped one little bit, he wouldn't make it to his first choice college. He'd given Bob such a hard time about his heavy backpack yesterday, ribbed him about his own lightweight pack, and bragged about how he was 'travelin' light'. Didn't seem so funny now, nope. Why hadn't he studied last night? Why hadn't he paid more attention in class?

Across the aisle, Bob zipped through the same test. *Boy, am I glad I studied!*, he thought. Glancing down and toward Ted, he saw the anxiety all over him. *I can't believe he asked me to cheat for him.* Bob still couldn't believe his best friend had asked him to do something like that.

A few weeks later, Bob got his college acceptance letter. He ran to show his folks, and they told him how proud of him they were. His dad's voice stopped him just as he was going to call Ted. "Son, wait a minute. **Don't call Ted just now, OK? I saw his dad today and he didn't make it.** Seems his grades were too low. They told him he could reapply next year, after he takes some remedial classes at the junior college. Wanted you to know before you see him, that's all."

* * * * * * * * * *

How prepared are you in your relationship with God? Your life as a disciple (learner) of Jesus Christ?

A strong, living, passionate relationship with God through Jesus will prepare you for whatever and wherever your life takes you.

Do you have 'extra oil for your lamp'? Is your spiritual life brimming full with God's grace?

Or like those foolish bridesmaids, is your lamp barely full? Do you have to shake it to tell if there's any spiritual fuel in there?**Is your spirit 'travelin' light'?**

Better 'fuel up'! Build your prayer life, get into Scripture, soak in some good Christian music. Who knows how much spiritual fuel you'll need today!

Reflections

What would real-life "extra oil for your lamp" look like?

What kind of spiritual "lamp oil" best fuels you? (perhaps prayer/God-time, reading/thinking about Scripture, or listening to Christian music?)

41

Heavenly Investment

"It's also like a man going on an extended trip. He called his servants together and delegated responsibilities. **To one he gave five thousand dollars, to another two thousand, to a third one thousand, depending on their abilities. Then he left.** *Right off, the first servant went to work and doubled his master's investment. The second did the same. But the man with the single thousand dug a hole and carefully buried his master's money.*

*"**After a long absence, the master of those three servants came back and settled up with them.** The one given five thousand dollars showed him how he had doubled his investment. His master commended him: 'Good work! You did your job well. From now on, be my partner.'*

"The servant with the two thousand showed how he also had doubled his master's investment. His master commended him: 'Good work! You did your job well. From now on, be my partner.'

*"**The servant given one thousand said,** 'Master, I know you have high standards and hate careless ways, that you demand the best and make no allowances for error. I was afraid I might disappoint you, so **I found a good hiding place and secured your money.** Here it is, safe and sound to the last cent.'*

*"**The master was furious. 'That's a terrible way to live! It's criminal to live cautiously like that!** If you knew I was after the best, why did you do less than the least? The least you could have done would have been to invest the sum with the bankers, where at least I would have gotten a little interest. **Take the thousand and give it to the one who risked the most.** And get rid of this play-it-safe who won't go out on a limb. Throw him into utter darkness.'"*

- Matthew 25: 14-20 (The Message Version)

* * * * * * * * * *

Quadruple bypass surgery. Not good news, and even worse timing. At 53 years old, Dale was in a real fix. **A third generation farmer,** he sat gazing out at one of his three large spreads of land. April. **Two weeks till planting time. The doctor said NOW.** He'd tried the 'how about in a month' thing. Answer: NOW.

Dale placed the first of three calls to his sons. "Sure, Dad, I'll help. How about if each of us takes a field? You know you'll be off your feet a good couple of months, right?" Dale's oldest, Tom was also the most practical and level headed – and the most likely to be SURE Dale took care of himself. "Dad," Tom calmly told him, "I want to keep you around. Our kids need their grandpa. You hear me, Dad?" "OK, OK, yeah, I hear you," came Dale's response.

"Dad, I'll call Brian and Chuck and let them know the plan. I'll get back to you. How about if we all go out for supper together? That way we can get our act together."

So the Bentley men gathered for t-bones and farm planning that night. Each son would take one of the three spreads. Seed and supplies had been ordered, received, and stored. All that was needed was hard work. Tom took the fields closest to the farmhouse, Brian, the middle son, chose the fields out across the creek, and Chuck (the 'city boy' who owned a motel in town) took the fields on the other side of town, closest to his house.

Dale had successful bypass surgery a week later. All three sons picked up their seed and supplies from the main barns. Weeks passed. Dale's recovery was slower than planned. April faded into May, and soon it was June, then the beginning of July. He watched the corn sprout and grow from his recliner by the big window. **He called all three sons and invited them and their families over for a July 4th potluck picnic.** *Wow,* Dale thought, *if the other two fields look like this one, this'll be a great season!*

Sitting around the traditional Bentley family July 4th bonfire later, **Dale asked his sons, "So, how's the corn doing? What's the harvest looking like?"**

Tom grinned. "Well Dad, you can see my part. I think it's going to be a great year. I'd say we'll **get more than double last year's crop from this field!"** Dale beamed. "I'm so proud of you, Tom!"

Attention turned to Brian. "Been a while since I farmed, Dad, but I think we might get double, maybe a little less. I've been asking around, tried a couple of new things..." Dale's eyes glistened as he looked at them. "You learned well, Brian. I hope I taught you that you've just gotta risk sometimes. **Good job, son!"**

Chuck was really squirming by now. The field he was in charge of was way on the other side of town. It was really just luck that neither of his brothers had been over there.

Dad's voice interrupted **Chuck's growing sense of dread.** "Well, Chuck? How's my businessman son's field doing?" Silence. Now all eyes were on Chuck.

"Well, you know there's a reason I'm not a farmer...." Silence. Everyone waited.
"I still have all the seed...it's safe in the barn over there. The farm supply guy says it'll grow good as new next season...I just knew, Dad, well, you're pretty tough on crop expectations, that's all."

"WHAT?" Dale's face grew red, then a dangerous sort of purple. Molly, his wife glared at her youngest son. **"You didn't. Chuck, tell me this is just one of your jokes, OK?"** Silence.....

"Dad, calm down, OK?" Tom was scared. **Dad didn't need this. What HAD Chuck been thinking?**

Molly got up and went behind Dale, laying a hand on his shoulder. "Honey, please..."
Tom spoke again, looking his dad straight in the eye. "Dad, remember what I told you? These kids need their grandpa. **I'll take care of this, OK? Chuck, Brian, let's take a little walk.**

Chuck went back to his motel managing. Brian and Tom took over the third field, planting late season crops to sell at the farmer's market. Their families helped harvest and run the stand at the market. Chuck mended his relationship with his dad and brothers, but Dad never trusted him with that much again. **Chuck learned a big, valuable lesson he passed on to his own children.**

* * * * * * * * * *

We are God's 'heavenly investment'. Just like the master in Jesus' story, God has heavily invested in our success as His children.

God has entrusted each of us, created in God's own image, with seeds of Christ's Good News. Each of us has our own 'field' to plant, care for, and grow. Like Dale, the dad in our story, God is there, right beside us. We can go to him for strength and wisdom.

Many times, we'll be like Chuck. We'll hide the seeds we've been entrusted with. The truth is, though, that those hidden seeds won't sprout, and they won't grow either. Harvest = zero.

Sometimes, we're like Brian. We're a bit (OK, sometimes a lot) afraid, but we sow those Good News seeds anyway. We try some new things, listen to more experienced 'seed planters', we work, and we pray. And hey, we actually get a decent harvest!

On our best (probably rarest) days, we're Good News farmers on the order of Tom. We just get out there in the field that God prepares for us. We plant, water, whatever it takes to be God's instrument of Good News, of the spreading of God's kingdom here on earth. When that happens, look out! The results will truly be amazing!

The truth is, God calls each of us to be 'Toms'. As we grow and mature in our faith, leaning and listening to God and those God sends into our lives to guide us, **we are transformed by Grace into....The Master's farmers!**

Reflections

What's your "field"? Where has God placed you?

Which son are you more like today? How can you tell?

42

Jesus-Blindness

"But **when the Son of Man comes in his glory**, and all the angels with him, then he will sit upon his glorious throne. All the nations will be gathered in his presence, and he will separate them as a shepherd separates the sheep from the goats.**He will place the sheep at his right hand and the goats at his left.**

"Then the **King will say to those on the right, 'Come, you who are blessed by my Father**, inherit the Kingdom prepared for you from the foundation of the world.For I was hungry, and you fed me. I was thirsty, and you gave me a drink. I was a stranger, and you invited me into your home.

I was naked, and you gave me clothing. I was sick, and you cared for me. I was in prison, and you visited me.'

"**Then these righteous ones will reply, 'Lord, when did we ever see you hungry and feed you? Or thirsty and give you something to drink?Or a stranger and show you hospitality? Or naked and give you clothing?When did we ever see you sick or in prison, and visit you?'**

"And the King will tell them, 'I assure you, **when you did it to one of the least of these my brothers and sisters, you were doing it to me!'**

"Then the King will turn to those on the left and say, '**Away with you, you cursed ones, into the eternal fire prepared for the Devil and his demons!For I was hungry, and you didn't feed me.** I was thirsty, and you didn't give me anything to drink.I was a stranger, and you didn't invite me into your home. I was naked, and you gave me no clothing. I was sick and in prison, and you didn't visit me.'

"Then they **will reply, 'Lord, when did we ever see you hungry or thirsty or a stranger or naked or sick or in prison, and not help you?'**

"And he will answer, '**I assure you, when you refused to help the least of these my brothers and sisters, you were refusing to help me.'**And they will go away into eternal punishment, but the righteous will go into eternal life."

- Matthew 25: 31-46 (New Living Translation)

* * * * * * * * * *

"Where's your Jesus <u>now</u>, little girl?" They taunted her, these big kids. She'd been swinging, just playing happily on the school playground. They'd come out of nowhere, grabbed her backpack (the new one with the pretty beaded cross on it) and started playing catch with it.

She looked around. No grown ups in sight. **Where <u>was</u> her big brother Joe?** He was supposed to meet her here fifteen minutes ago.

"Yeah, tell <u>Jesus</u> to come get your backpack – like He cares!" They kept tossing it back and forth, letting it land in the dirt each time. Molly was afraid she'd be next. She looked around frantically as they moved closer and closer to her.

"So, baby girl, is Jesus in here? They ripped open her backpack, scattering her school papers all over the ground. Molly's small pink leather Bible fell out – the one her grandmother had given her last Christmas. One of the big kids picked it up.

"You actually <u>read </u>this?", he asked her. She nodded, her throat too dry and her mouth too scared shut to say the 'yes' she was thinking.

"So where does <u>it</u> tell you Jesus is?" The mean boy looked her right in the eye.

"The Bible tells me Jesus is in everybody I meet. I guess that includes you. I sure <u>hope</u> it does anyway." The words just sort of popped out of her. Fear and dread filled her insides like lead as the boy came closer and closer. He reached out and stopped her swing.

Then came the biggest surprise of her young life. He handed her the Bible and turned to his buddies. "Hey this is no fun – she's just a little kid. What's the challenge in that? Let's go; I'll catch up with you in a minute."

As the others left, he picked up her backpack and started stuffing the papers he could still find into it. Molly sat frozen in place on the swing, wondering what he was going to do. "Here, little girl. Hey, you shouldn't be here by yourself, you know? And I hope you're right – I hope I can find this Jesus too. See ya." And with that, he was gone.

* * * * * * * * *

"Mrs. Simpson? Mrs. Simpson! The recess bell rang; isn't it time for us to line up?" The young voice snapped Molly back to today, to the reality of her students waiting for her to take them back inside the old school building. Funny how memories are.

For a minute it felt like that day so many years ago, right on this very playground. Funny how God had used that day to open up His call on her life. She'd really been blind until that day – blind to all the places Jesus <u>really</u> could be found – if she just looked. 'Jesus-blindness', that's what her grandmother had called it.

That evening at parent-teacher conferences, she thought she recognized the young father as he walked into her classroom. "Bet you don't remember me, do you?", he asked. There was something about him, something familiar, but she just couldn't place it.

He smiled. "I brought you something. I've had it for a long time, ever since I was a wild teenager terrorizing little kids on the playground – that playground right out there." He reached into his wallet and took out a worn little card.

Tears came to her eyes as he handed her the card. The words of 'Jesus Loves Me, This I Know' were on one side, and a little note from her grandmother was on the back. "Honey," it read, "Look for Jesus everywhere you go, because He's already there, and he's waiting to touch everyone you meet. Love you baby. Grandma"

"**Mrs. Simpson, you'll never know how much you and your little card changed my life.** I found it after you left that day. A week later, some guys beat me up and left me for dead. They took my wallet, and I don't know to this day how it happened, but **this card was the only thing they found in my pocket.** The nurses, they assumed I was a Christian, so they called the chaplain. Funny thing, he saw Jesus in me too – just like you did. I just want to thank you. And my little girl, well, you gotta know she loves you like crazy too."

* * * * * * * * * *

How will you meet Jesus today? Tomorrow?
How will God touch others with Jesus through you today? Tomorrow?

All of us suffer from 'Jesus-blindness'. Every last one. That's why we're created to live in community, each one showing another Jesus and the awesomeness of God's grace.

We're all hungry, thirsty, naked, imprisoned – in some way. Sometimes it's more obvious, sometimes not.

And Jesus? Well, He's in all those hard-to-believe-He'd-ever-be-HERE kind of people and places, with us, before us, after us. **Just when you might least expect it.....THERE HE IS!!**

Can you see Him?

Reflections

Where are some surprising places or people you've "seen Jesus" in?

How would you define "Jesus-blindness"?

43

Anonymous Extravagance

When Jesus had finished saying these things, he said to his disciples, "As you know, the Passover celebration begins in two days, and I, the Son of Man, will be betrayed and crucified."

*At that same time the **leading priests and other leaders were meeting** at the residence of Caiaphas, the high priest, **to discuss how to capture Jesus secretly and put him to death.** "But not during the Passover," they agreed, "or there will be a riot."*

*Meanwhile, **Jesus was in Bethany** at the home of Simon, a man who had leprosy. During supper, **a woman came in with a beautiful jar of expensive perfume and poured it over his head.***

*The disciples were indignant when they saw this. **"What a waste of money," they said.** "She could have sold it for a fortune and given the money to the poor."*

*But Jesus replied, "Why berate her for doing such a good thing to me? You will always have the poor among you, but I will not be here with you much longer. She has poured this perfume on me to prepare my body for burial. **I assure you, wherever the Good News is preached throughout the world, this woman's deed will be talked about in her memory.""***

- *Matthew 26: 1-13 (New Living Translation)*

* * * * * * * * *

"I wish I knew his name." He paused for a moment. "You know, I've never forgotten him, never forgotten his face. God knows who he is, but I sure wish I did. **You asked me what my most memorable event was in my over 30 years as a cop, and here it is."**

"I remember it like it was yesterday. I was new on the beat, just a rookie in the worst part of town. You could say I was in the dark in more than one way that night. I didn't even know what was going down, not till this **homeless, nameless kid screamed 'Get down'. I remember him running in front of me,** remember diving for the sidewalk, remember the shots, remember the blood all over the place."

"That kid didn't even know me. Worse yet, cops weren't real popular in that neighborhood, you know? Before I knew it, my partner was there, medics were on the scene, and I figured out most of that blood wasn't mine. That kid, he couldn't have been more than fourteen years old. He gave his life up for me, a cop – a guy he didn't even know, and probably never even saw before."

He pulled an old, worn picture out of his wallet. **"I call him Jimmy."** Cameras zoomed in on the picture. **"We never found out his name, but I'll never forget his face.** This whole thing today, the party, **this wonderful retirement celebration – I want you to know it's in memory of him."**

Few eyes were dry by this time as he raised his glass and looked heavenward. **"Bless you, Jimmy, and thanks for blessing me with such an extravagant gift – the gift of a lifetime."**

* * * * * * * * * *

Did you know that Jesus suffered and died – for people who didn't even know Him? For generations of people not even born yet? Now that's the tops of anonymous extravagance! How many of us would do that?

And what about this woman with the expensive perfumed oil? How much food could she have provided for her family if she'd sold it? Why WOULD she 'waste it' on Jesus' head? What if it was all she had? Never mind the objections of the disciples; what about her family? Can't you just hear it now: "So, what did you get for that expensive oil at market? What did you bring home for us? You did WHAT with it? You KNOW he's trouble, that 'Jesus'! And you did WHAT?"

Anonymous extravagance. Jimmy did it. The woman with the oil did it. Jesus WAS God in living, breathing, loving extravagance. How about us?

How do we live our lives in the light of God's 'anonymous extravagance'? How do we respond to His amazing grace given for us – even before we were born?

Let's spread Jesus' anonymous extravagance – everywhere we go and in every company we keep!

Reflections

Why do you think it's hard for people to serve and give to others anonymously?

Think of some ways you could respond to God's "anonymous extravagance" in the gift of Jesus the Christ......

44

Oh NO, Not ME!

Then Judas Iscariot, one of the twelve disciples, went to the leading priestsand asked, **"How much will you pay me to betray Jesus to you?" And they gave him thirty pieces of silver.***From that time on, Judas began looking for the right time and place to betray Jesus.*

On the first day of the Festival of Unleavened Bread, the disciples came to Jesus and asked, "Where do you want us to prepare the Passover supper?""As you go into the city," he told them, "you will see a certain man. Tell him, **'The Teacher says, My time has come, and I will eat the Passover meal with my disciples at your house.'"**

*So the disciples did as Jesus told them and prepared the Passover supper there.When it was evening, Jesus sat down at the table with the twelve disciples.***While they were eating, he said, "The truth is, one of you will betray me."***Greatly distressed, one by one they began to ask him,* <u>*"I'm not the one, am I, Lord?"*</u>

<u>*He replied, "One of you who is eating with me now will betray me.For I, the Son of Man, must die, as the Scriptures declared long ago. But* **how terrible it will be for my betrayer. Far better for him if he had never been born!"***</u>

Judas, the one who would betray him, also asked, <u>*"Teacher, I'm not the one, am I?"* *And Jesus told him,* **"You have said it yourself."**</u>

- Matthew 26: 14-25 (New Living Translation)

* * * * * * * * * *

"I <u>know</u> one of you has it."
Silence.

"I'll repeat. I <u>KNOW</u> one of <u>YOU</u> has it."
Silence – the kind that seems to stretch out....until itjust has to snap, like a jumbo rubber band strained beyond its limit. Then....SNAP!

A small hand shot up. **"Well, it wasn't <u>ME</u>!** I was in the bathroom, and before that I wasat the nurse's, and before that...anyway, why should <u>I</u> have to miss recess?"

The teacher'sglancetraveled around the classroom, resting on the pretty bright yellow dress. Hethought back, remembering the streak of bright yellow he'd seen as he stepped back into the classroom minutes before. **True, Millie<u>had</u> been out of the room – to the office, the nurse, and the bathroom, but....**

131

Five dollars. Just for the answers to the math test. It seemed so simple this morning when Tess asked her. But now.... Millie could feel the sweat trickle down her back.

"You know," Mr. Jenkins' mind was spinning now. *What to do?* "When we take things that aren't ours, **when wedo things we know are wrong....well kids, it all kind of falls in on us.** It's justnot worth it. Like I said, I KNOW one of you has that answer sheet. We're all going to recess now, but I want you to think about this really hard."

The kids all filed out to the playground. **Millie caught up with Tess by thetetherball courts. "Hey, I don't want this any more."** She reached in her pocket for the five dollar bill. Tess sneered at her. "I knew you were just a BABY. **Too late now!"**

Millie held the money out. "Here. It's not worth it. **I mean it – take it back."** With that, she threw the five dollars at Tess's feet and ran back into the school building, Tess hot on her heels.

Running through the doors at full speed, with Tess just a step behind, **Millie ran smack into Mr. Jenkins.** "Whoa there! What's wrong?"Tess, having come to a screeching halt right outside the doors, melted back outside, headed for the closest group of kids to blend in (and look as innocent as possible).

Mr. Jenkins put his hands on Millie's shoulders, steadying her as her breath came in quick gasps. **"Millie, are you OK? What's wrong?"** As her eyes met his, she knew, just KNEW Mr. Jenkins already had it figured out – at least her part.

"I'm so sorry," she blurted out as the tears began to drip down her face.

"I know, Millie. But you realize it's too late, don't you?" All the kids have taken that test, and there's no way for me to know who got those answers and who didn't. I'll have to give everyone a whole new test now. Do you understand that?" He knelt down, his eyes level with hers.

"Yyyeeess," slipped from Millie in the middle of her sniffles, **"But once I did it, I didn't know how to take it back!"**

* * * * * * * * *

Like Judas, we'd all like to say, "Oh no, not me!", but the truth is that often it IS us. It's us who speak and act in ways that betray Christ. **It's us that forget who – and Whose – we really are.**

Many times we think it's too late (just like Judas). How could Jesus want to claim us as His disciples after...... (fill in the blank)?

Just as JesusKnew Judas' heart, and temptations, so He knows ours. **Just as Jesus loved Judas**, soHe loves us. We follow a Master who knows the power of temptation intimately. He's been there.

I'm always amazed that **Jesus washed ALL the disciples' feet, eventhose of Judas**, whom he knew would betray him. He knew Judas would sell Jesus' very life for a mere bunch of silver coins. And still....

Millie was my neighbor. She got off the school bus that day and came to me while I was in my front yard weeding flowers. **We talked for a long while – about weeds** – in my flowers and in life. Weeds grew, but had to be pulled out so the flowers could grow. **That day Millie pulled a weed out of her life.** That day she learned that God loved her even when she made big mistakes. That day Millie grew a lot closer to God, and **came even closer to understanding the heart of Jesus.**

The next Sunday her whole family came to our church. Two weeks later Millie came forward in worship to claim Jesus as her Lord and Savior. Through her testimony, her parents came too.

They'd been out of church for ten years. Her dad put it best when he said, "Tried it before. Seemed like it was only for perfect people, and God knows that's not us. We needed real church, a real God, for the real world we live in. I think we've found it, and Him, here."

How about you? Made mistakes too? Well, Jesus died to show you just how much He loves you – the real you. **He would've washed your feet too, you know. Really.**

Reflections

How would you describe a "real church"?

How does God meet you in the "real world" of your life?

What would you say to someone who had made a big mistake and thought it was too late for Christ to help them, for them to be accepted and loved by God?

45

Real Food

While they were eating, Jesus took a loaf of bread, and **after blessing it he broke it, gave it to the disciples, and said, "Take, eat; this is my body."**

Then he took a cup, and after giving thanks he gave it to them, saying, **"Drink from it, all of you; for this is my blood of the covenant, which is poured out for many for the forgiveness of sins.**

I tell you, I will never again drink of this fruit of the vine until that day when I drink it new with you in my Father's kingdom."

When they had sung the hymn, they went out to the Mount of Olives.

- *Matthew 26: 26-30 (New Revised Standard Version)*

During the meal, Jesus took and **blessed the bread, broke it, and gave it to His disciples: "Take, eat. This is my body."**

Taking the cup and thanking God, he gave it to them: **"Drink this, all of you. This is my blood, God's new covenant poured out for many people for the forgiveness of sins."**

"I'll not be drinking wine from this cup again until that new day when I'll drink it with you in the kingdom of my Father."
They sang a hymn and went directly to Mount Olives.

- *Matthew 26: 26-30 (The Message Version)*

* * * * * * * * * *

It was her intense concentration on the menu that caught my attention. I'd never seen a small child look so intently at the choices. She looked, and looked some more. She turned the menu over. She turned it upside down. Then she sighed – you know, that exasperated, 'had enough of this' kind of sigh. "What is it, Molly?", her dad asked. "Have you decided what you're having?"

His questions were greeted with...another sigh, and – silence.

"Honey, look here. They have hamburgers, chicken fingers, grilled cheese....and look – nachos!"
Molly closed the menu. **"Don't they have any REAL food here, Dad?"**

"Like I said, honey, they have real hamburgers, real chicken fingers, real grilled cheese sandwiches, and REAL nachos! Which will it be?"

"Da-a-ad! I'm looking for that 'real food' Pastor Pat told us about this morning. Remember? She said it's the best food ever, 'cause it's forever food! Don't you remember? It was on the Jesus-Table. It's GOT to be here somewhere." She opened the menu again, searching with her finger.

Dad smiled, you got it, that 'oh my, what do I say to that' kind of smile. "Well, honey, they only have that kind of food at church. **Here we eat regular food."**

"Oh no, Dad. **Jesus isn't just at church. He's EVERYwhere, even here in this restaurant.** So where's the REAL food, the Jesus-food?"

Dad reached across the table and closed Molly's menu. Looking her straight in the eye, love shining in his face, he told her, **"Sweetheart, it's inside you. When we share that 'real food', the 'Jesus-meal' at His Table, it sticks with us all week.** You're right, it's the most real food there is, and it lasts forever. We go back each week to church and share it with Jesus and it just gets better and better, and we get stronger and stronger." He paused, amazed that she was still gazing back at him, not missing one word. Then all of a sudden, a big bright smile just blossomed on her face.

"I get it! We just get more and more filled up with Jesus, and we grow stronger and stronger inside, and that makes God REAL happy!!"

"OK, Dad. I'll have a cheese sandwich. **We're going to church next week, right? Pastor Pat said she misses me when I'm not there, and I think Jesus does too. Right, Dad?"**

Dad smiled. "Right, honey. You are SO right!"

* * * * * * * * *

Sometimes we get so 'fed-up' in the world, stuffed full with the 'food' of just living day to day, that we forget about the eternal food Jesus offers. We eat at table after table. We fill our time with this and that, that and this. Over and over again. Sooner or later, we realize something's missing. Something REAL. Something beyond all that everyday stuff.

Our menu is full, but there's nothing on there we really need, nothing there that will truly give us the nourishment, the energy and power we need to truly LIVE life to the fullest potential God intends us to. God created us for joyful, grace-filled living in the Light and Way of His Son, Jesus, who offered His entire self as REAL food. His Body. His Blood. For us. REAL food, for REAL people.

So how about it?

Reflections

How is Communion, the Lord's Supper, different from "regular food" for you?

What kind of things do people fill their lives with that seems to leave no room for the "real food" of the Lord's Supper?

What would you tell Molly?

46

Promises, Promises...

*Then Jesus said to them, "You will all become deserters because of me this night; for it is written, 'I will strike the shepherd, and the sheep of the flock will be scattered.' **But after I am raised up, I will go ahead of you to Galilee.'***
*Peter said to him, "Though all become deserters because of you, **I will never desert you."***
Jesus said to him, "Truly I tell you, this very night, before the cock crows, you will deny me three times."
Peter said to him, "Even though I must die with you, I will not deny you." And so said all the disciples.
– Matthew 26: 31-35 (New Revised Standard Version)

*Jesus said to his disciples, "During this very night, all of you will reject me, as the Scriptures say, 'I will strike down the shepherd, and the sheep will be scattered.' **But after I am raised to life, I will go to Galilee ahead of you."***
*Peter spoke up, **"Even if all the others reject you, I never will!"***
Jesus replied, "I promise you that before a rooster crows tonight, you will say three times that you don't know me." But Peter said, "Even if I have to die with you, I will never say I don't know you." All the others said the same thing.
– Matthew 26: 31-35 (Contemporary English Version)

* * * * * * * * * *

Will watched the strange car pull into their long, winding driveway from his hideaway in the attic of their old farmhouse. He squinted his eyes, **trying to read the odd license plate**, but all he knew was it wasn't the kind he saw every day as his mom drove him to school in town.

He could hear the gravel crunch under the tires as the car pulled up in front of the big porch that wrapped around the house. **Uniforms!** Just like his brother Roy wore! Maybe, if these guys were home, Roy was too! Yippee! Will scurried down the steps. "Mom! Mom! There's soldiers here! **Maybe they're Roy's buddies!"**

Mom was vacuuming as Will came running through the living room. Just as she shut off the vacuum to see why he was so excited, **the doorbell rang. Their lives would never be the same.**

Will saw the sudden panic cross his mom's face, and it puzzled him – for a minute. Seeing his mom frozen, staring out the window at the approaching men, he opened the door. **"Did you bring my brother home too? Is** he with you?" Will peered around the soldiers, looking for Roy's bright blond hair. Nothing. Just the two guys standing on the porch, their eyes filling with tears as they looked at him and mom.

"Ma'am, we're sorry, but..." With that, his mom collapsed onto the sofa, and Will knew. But it just couldn't be. He remembered the night before Roy left, how he'd been so worried, because this wasn't like those video games some of his friends played. Nope, this was real. But his big brother had held him tight in one of his famous dare-you-to-get-out-of-this bear hugs. Roy's words came swimming back through his memory, just like it was yesterday. **"Hey, Little Will,"** That was Roy's special name for Will, ever since he was born when Roy was eight years old. **"You know I'll never leave you. Never. You hear me?"**

Yeah, right.

Reality hit 10 year old Will like a sledge hammer. **"But he PROMISED he'd come home. He PROMISED he'd never leave me!"**

"I bet you're Will, right?" The young corporal's voice gently spoke into the silence. Will nodded. "Well, Will, a **young friend of your brother's sent this picture for you.** It has a message on the back. He had one of our translators write it for him. Your brother saved his life." The young man reached into his pocket and pulled out a worn, wrinkled photograph. "Here, son. This is for you. His name's Niso. **That's him, standing next to your brother."**

Will gazed at the picture for a long minute, tears streaming down his face, bouncing off the edge of it and onto his lap. **"Will, Niso seemed sure you'd understand what your brother's message meant. They were his last words, Will.** Roy saw the trip wire at the last second and shoved Niso clear. Oh, there was one other thing. The translator said **Niso wanted to be sure you knew that Roy taught him about Jesus. His exact words were, 'Roy gave me Jesus'.**

Will slowly turned the photo over, not really wanting to stop looking at his brother's face. The message read, **"Even though you can't see me, I'll still never leave you. I'll be in that little piece of Jesus in your heart. Love you, Little Will. Remember Matthew 26:32.**
Love, Roy"

* * * * * * * * *

All of us have crisis times in our lives. People we thought we could count on don't come through. Things we've planned for don't work out. **Like Will, our hearts cry out.** It's especially in those times that we need the 'Roys' in our lives, to 'give us Jesus'. We need to know that in fact, **Jesus will never, ever leave us,** even in those times when we don't think we can see Him.

Will shared his 'traveling picture gallery' of his brother with me. He calls it...are you ready? "Galilee, Matthew 26:32"

Remember: His promise is real. His promise is true.

Reflections

How do you react when someone promises you something and it doesn't happen? What carries you through?

How about when you can't follow through with a promise you've made to someone?

47

Soooooo Sleeeeepy...

Then Jesus brought them to an olive grove called Gethsemane, and he said, "Sit here while I go on ahead to pray."

He took Peter and Zebedee's two sons, James and John, and he began to be filled with anguish and deep distress.He told them, "My soul is crushed with grief to the point of death. Stay here and watch with me."

He went on a little farther and fell face down on the ground, praying, "My Father! If it is possible, let this cup of suffering be taken away from me. Yet I want your will, not mine."

*Then **he returned to the disciples and found them asleep.** He said to Peter, "Couldn't you stay awake and watch with me even one hour?Keep alert and pray. Otherwise temptation will overpower you. For **though the spirit is willing enough, the body is weak!"***

Again he left them and prayed, "My Father! If this cup cannot be taken away until I drink it, your will be done."

*He returned to them **again and found them sleeping**, for they just couldn't keep their eyes open.So he went back to pray **a third time**, saying the same things again.*

*Then he came to the disciples and said, **"Still sleeping?** Still resting? Look, the time has come. I, the Son of Man, am betrayed into the hands of sinners.Up, let's be going. See, my betrayer is here!"*

- Matthew 26: 36-46 (New Living Translation)

*Then Jesus went with them to a garden called Gethsemane and told his disciples, **"Stay here while I go over there and pray."** Taking along Peter and the two sons of Zebedee, he plunged into an agonizing sorrow. Then he said, "This sorrow is crushing my life out. Stay here and keep vigil with me."*

Going a little ahead, he fell on his face, praying, "My Father, if there is any way, get me out of this. But please, not what I want. You, what do you want?"

***When he came back to his disciples, he found them sound asleep.** He said to Peter, "Can't you stick it out with me a single hour? Stay alert; be in prayer so you don't wander into temptation without even knowing you're in danger. There is a part of you that is eager, ready for anything in God. But there's another part that's as lazy as an old dog sleeping by the fire."*

He then left them a second time. Again he prayed, "My Father, if there is no other way than this, drinking the cup to the dregs, I'm ready. Do it your way."

***When he came back, he again found them sound asleep.** They simply couldn't keep their eyes open. This time he let them sleep on, and went back a third time to pray, going over the same ground one last time.*

***When he came back the next time, he said,** "Are you going to sleep on and make a night of it? My time is up, the Son of Man is about to be handed over to the hands of sinners. **Get up! Let's get going!** My betrayer is here."*

- Matthew 26: 36-46 (The Message Version)

* * * * * * * * * *

Seventeen years. Count them, seventeen. That's how much of his life Pete had given to the company. All for what? **"Downsizing",** they'd told him as they laid him off. Yeah, right. With two kids in college and a mortgage to pay, **how was HE supposed to "downsize"** (more like 'outsize' was his thought)?

The **bills just kept coming,** day after day, more and more. Then came the phone calls – morning, noon, and night they came. He didn't even answer the phone any more unless he knew exactly who was calling (and he thanked God daily for caller ID).

Bad news, and more bad news. The 'bill basket' was overflowing. The files where he kept the bills were overcrowded. And still the envelopes kept arriving. **They all wanted what Pete didn't have – money.**

Just as he was praying for deliverance – any kind of deliverance – more mail dropped through the mail slot in the front door, cascading onto the floor. Thank goodness it was Thursday – almost the end of the week. **At least no bad news came through the mail slot on Sundays. These days he appreciated Sundays more than he figured he ever had in his life.**

Pete bent down (easier these days since he'd lost weight – funny what good can come from buying less food) and retrieved the mess of mail. Bill, bill, bill, advertisement (what, didn't they know he had NO money?). He took the stack over to his desk to sort it all out. **Bills – in the basket. Ads – in the trash can. That was it.**

Pete decided to go for a walk. It had become a daily habit. Every day after the mail came, Pete took off on what he called **his daily "Help Me Jesus Prayer Walk".** As he walked, he fervently prayed for God to help him out of this mess. I mean, really, what had he done to deserve THIS?

Friday came. More mail. Bills – in the basket. Ads – in the trash. As he stuffed the bills into the basket, a couple fell out onto the floor. Hmmm. **This one looked odd, different.** Probably just some trick to get him to open another 'pay up or else' letter. **Pete rammed it deep into the bill basket.** THAT one would stay put until he was good and ready to open it!

Out the door for the daily "Help Me Jesus Prayer Walk" he went.

Saturday arrived, bright and sunny. Good thing too, because the electric would be shut off today. At least it would be warmer today so Pete could open the windows and let the warm breeze to blow through.

Click. Swish. Plop. **Great, more mail.** He picked them up and headed for his desk. Bills – in the basket (took some muscle by this time to fit them all in). Ads – in the trash.

Ah – something else – **a birthday card from his oldest daughter, Sue.** Pete settled in, a smile on his face and a tear in his eye, to read the card. Sue always remembered his birthday. As he opened the card, a five dollar bill fell out. "Dad," she'd written, "I know it's not much, but I love you. I hope this helps somehow."

As Pete reached over to pin the beautiful card to his bulletin board, **a couple of those pesky bills fell out of the basket. Again, with that funny looking one! Growling, Pete grabbed it and rammed it back into the basket.** *Take that, you!* He thought to himself as he got up and headed out the door for his walk.

Thank God tomorrow would be Sunday. Church. Friends. And get this – NO MAIL. NO BILLS!

Sunday arrived, bright and sunny. As his friend Rod dropped him back in front of his house after church (no money for gas these days), **he headed for that bill basket.** Sorting. Pitching. Sorting. Pitching. He got out his checkbook to pay what he could, wrote the checks, sealed them up, filed the rest.

Pete started to get up when **his eye fell on the crumpled mess in the bottom of the bill basket.** Oh yes. That weird looking envelope. OK, he might as well open one more.Pete stood at his desk, ripping open the envelope – but **swiftly fell back into his chair** as he looked again at the contents of that strange envelope. Not a bill, nope. **A check fell out.** A check for.....$10,000! Was it real, or was this **someone's idea of a sick joke?**

He took a deep breath the next morning as he took his daily "Help Me Jesus Prayer Walk" early, heading for the bank. **Emily, his favorite bank teller, grinned as he presented the check.** "Hey Emily," Pete began. Emily's eyes widened as she noticed the amount of the check. "OK Mr. Jeffs, I know you. **I bet you want to know if it's real, right?"** Relieved, he answered, "Well, just don't arrest me if it's not, OK? It came in the mail, and **I don't even know the folks who sent it."**

Emily stepped away from the counter and went to the phone. She returned a few minutes later. **"Seems you made an impression on this lady,"** she began as she pushed a slip of paper across the counter with a name written on it – Lucille Johnson.

Pete stared at the name. It looked familiar. Oh my gosh! Why it'd been years! He remembered now – she used to live down the street. Her husband had been killed in an accident and Pete had done her yard work until she'd moved to an apartment a few months later.

Emily interrupted his trip down memory lane. **"Mr. Jeffs? Did you see this note taped to the back?"** Well of course he hadn't – he'd been shocked enough about the front of the check! She turned the check over and peeled off the sticky-note.

"Get up and get GOING!!" was what it said. And Pete did just that.

* * * * * * * * * *

So here's a question. **Why did the disciples stay?** I mean, why not just go home, if they're really that tired? They're not too helpful to Jesus anyway.

Here's a better question. **Why did Jesus keep coming back** to the disciples? I mean, why not just send them home, if they're that tired? They're not too helpful to Him anyway.

Why didn't Pete just throw that envelope away with the rest? Why did it keep 'popping out' of that bill basket?

Even after Peter, James and John fail their 'assignment' repeatedly, **Jesus still returns.** More than that, **He still wants them with Him,** after all that! "Get up!", He tells them that last time, "Let's get going!"

Like that envelope, Jesus keeps 'popping up' in our lives. He NEVER gives up. Do we fail? Yep. Do we let Him down? Repeatedly.

We are often 'asleep at the wheel' of life. Good thing our Lord and Savior isn't!

May we be more and more open to Jesus in our lives.
May we notice, hear, and obey His call on our lives – every day.
May we too, like the original disciples –

Wake up! Get up!And get going – with Jesus!!

Reflections

What does living life "asleep at the wheel" look like?

What difference could (or does) living with our eyes and ears open for Jesus' presence in our lives look like?

How are we like these original disicples?

Think of and/or share a time when Jesus has "popped up" in your life.

48

Kiss of Death?

And even as he said this, Judas, one of the twelve disciples, arrived with a mob that was armed with swords and clubs. They had been sent out by the leading priests and other leaders of the people. **Judas had given them a prearranged signal: "You will know which one to arrest when I go over and give him the kiss of greeting."**

So Judas came straight to Jesus. "Greetings, Teacher!" he exclaimed and gave him the kiss.

Jesus said, "My friend, go ahead and do what you have come for." Then the others grabbed Jesus and arrested him.

One of the men with Jesus pulled out a sword and slashed off an ear of the high priest's servant. "Put away your sword," Jesus told him. "Those who use the sword will be killed by the sword. Don't you realize that I could ask my Father for thousands of angels to protect us, and he would send them instantly? But if I did, how would the Scriptures be fulfilled that describe what must happen now?"

Then Jesus said to the crowd, "Am I some dangerous criminal, that you have come armed with swords and clubs to arrest me? Why didn't you arrest me in the Temple? I was there teaching every day. But this is all happening to fulfill the words of the prophets as recorded in the Scriptures." **At that point, all the disciples deserted him and fled.**

- Matthew 26: 47-56 (New Living Translation)

The words were barely out of his mouth when Judas (the one from the Twelve) showed up, and with him a gang from the high priests and religious leaders brandishing swords and clubs. The **betrayer had worked out a sign with them, "The one I kiss, that's the one – seize him." He went straight to Jesus, greeted him, "How are you, Rabbi?" and kissed him.**

Jesus said, "Friend, why this charade?"

Then they came on him – grabbed him and roughed him up. One of those with Jesus pulled his sword and, taking a swing at the Chef Priest's servant, cut off his ear.

Jesus said, "Put your sword back where it belongs. All who use swords are destroyed by swords. Don't you realize that I am able right now to call to my father, and twelve companies – more, if I want them – of fighting angels would be here, battle-ready? But if I did that, how would the Scriptures come true that say this is the way it has to be?"

Then Jesus addressed the mob: "What is this – coming out after me with swords and clubs as if I were a dangerous criminal? Day after day I have been sitting in the Temple teaching, and you never so much as lifted a hand against me. You've done it this way to confirm and fulfill the prophetic writings." **Then all the disciples cut and ran.**

– Matthew 26: 47-56 (The Message Version)

* * * * * * * * * *

"Oh man, getting HER as your lab partner is a kiss of death – kiss your biology 'A' goodbye, buddy."Theirs had been the last names called as lab partners were announced on the first day of class.

Yep. The new kid – and the 'kiss of death' partner. Story was, **she'd blown up a lab table** last semester in chemistry lab. It definitely seemed dangerous to hang out with HER in any kind of lab!

* * * * * * * * * *

"Hey, Phillip, are you still hanging out with that Jesus? Don't you know how dangerous it is even to be seen with him? Why, it could easily get you killed! You know, Phillip, rumor is that Judas guy's already sold him out. They're saying he's bringing the soldiers to arrest him – wonder what the signal's gonna be. I mean, will he just point to Jesus, or what?"

Hours later, Phillip saw....the kiss of death. And he ran.

* * * * * * * * * *

Tension was in the air as they all moved to their assigned lab stations, and there were more than a few glances at them as they took their seats.

"Thanks for....well....for not making a big deal..." Mara stammered, almost under her breath. "I mean... ummm.....I know you've heard about last semester..." The teacher looked their way, but Mara continued, **"Well, Tony, if you run too, I'll understand, really I will."**

After class, several of the guys gathered around Tony, each sympathizing with how he'd gotten 'stuck' with 'kiss of death' girl, each offering suggestions to help him get a new partner.

* * * * * * * * * *

Philip figured he'd never forget that instant. It was frozen in time, etched in his mind. The instant Judas' lips touched Jesus' cheek. The kiss of death.

Oh yeah, Philip ran. But then he thought. He prayed. And he returned – a stronger disciple than he'd ever been before.

And yes, they did arrest Jesus. They tortured Him. They killed Him. But **that never stopped Jesus – He came back.**

So did Philip.

* * * * * * * * * *

Tony was tempted. In fact, he 'missed' lab twice after that first day.

But then he saw Mara in the hall. "Hey Tony, guess what?" A big smile lit her face. This didn't look anything like the Mara he'd sat with in biology lab the other day! Did she have a twin or something?

Her excitement bubbled over. **"Just wanted to let you know – WE made an 'A' on the first lab!"** Tony and Mara went on to earn the highest grade in biology that year.

A year later, they shared the salutatorian honors at graduation, and **a year after** that they were married. At the wedding reception, Tony stood, tears in his eyes.

"I guess you could say that this 'kiss of death' woman has really been the beginning of a whole new life for me – a whole new, incredible life!"

* * * * * * * * * *

Both Phillip and Tony ran.
Both failed to 'stick with it'

Jesus never ran. Even in the face of betrayal. Even in the face of that 'kiss of death', Jesus showed that death is never the last word.

Hear Jesus as He tells you too –
You may run. You may fail.
But always remember, I'm running right beside you, and I'm waiting at the end of your run.
I'll lead you through failure to victory.

My child, let the kiss of death I received become the Gift of eternal life for you –
the Kiss of Life – eternal Life!

Reflections

What difference does (would) knowing that Jesus runs beside you in the race of life and waits to lead you to eternal victory and life mean to you?

How does (would) it change the way you live your life?

49

On Trial...Who, ME?

Then **the people who had arrested Jesus led him to the home of Caiaphas**, the high priest, where the teachers of religious law and other leaders had gathered.

Meanwhile, Peter was following far behind and eventually came to the courtyard of the high priest's house. He went in, sat with the guards, and waited to see what was going to happen to Jesus.

Inside, the leading priests and the entire high council were trying to find witnesses who would lie about Jesus, so they could put him to death. But even though they found many who agreed to give false witness, **there was no testimony they could use.**

Finally, two men were found who declared, "This man said, 'I am able to destroy the Temple of God and rebuild it in three days.'"

Then the high priest stood up and said to Jesus, "Well, aren't you going to answer these charges? What do you have to say for yourself?"

But Jesus remained silent. Then the high priest said to him, "I demand in the name of the living God that you tell us whether you are the Messiah, the Son of God."

Jesus replied, "Yes, it is as you say. And in the future you will see me, the Son of Man, sitting at God's right hand in the place of power and coming back on the clouds of heaven."

Then the high priest tore his clothing to show his horror, shouting, "Blasphemy! Why do we need other witnesses? You have all heard his blasphemy. What is your verdict?" "Guilty!" they shouted. "He must die!" Then they spit in Jesus' face and hit him with their fists. And some slapped him, saying, "Prophesy to us, you Messiah! Who hit you that time?"

- Matthew 26: 57-68 (New Living Translation)

* * * * * * * * * *

They'd found stolen merchandise in her break room locker. Tina knew she hadn't put it there, but what could she do now?

So **here she sat across the desk from the store manager.**

"Well, what do you have to say for yourself?" He looked her straight in the eye, his decision about her clear as the sun at midday (and just as hot).

What COULD she say?

The manager continued his tirade. "**We KNOW you did it. Just make it easy on yourself** and admit it." He looked at her again, waiting, tapping his fingers on the edge of his desk.

How was she supposed to admit to something she didn't do?

He sighed, exasperated. **"OK missy, here's the deal. We don't NEED any witnesses.** The evidence is clear, and the cops are on the way. This is your last chance to come clean!"

Tina finally had enough. Scared and angry, she spoke up.
"You said it. You obviously believe it. What can I possibly say? But soon You'll see for yourself - I AM innocent."
The manager, now way ready to be done with Tina, stood up to let **the police officer into the room.**

"She's all yours. Maybe you can get her to come to her senses. We took everything from her locker as evidence. Here." He handed the cop a big bag and turned his attention to the papers on his desk.

"OK, miss. Let's get this over with. The click of the handcuffs closing around her wrists was a sound Tina reckoned she'd never forget if she lived to be 100. "This way please." And with that, the officer led her through the store. How embarrassing.

Two long days later, as Tina sat in jail, more stolen items were found - in her break room locker. She was immediately freed. No apologies. No job back. But freedom sure felt good.

* * * * * * * * *

The 'evidence' was clear to them.
Jesus was accused - and convicted - based on the 'evidence'.

What could He say? The Truth.
What DID He say? The Truth.

They convicted Him.
They sentenced Him.
They killed Him.

And....He was freed – amazingly, completely, eternally!

So, **when you stand for Christ, the whole world might convict you.** The 'evidence' should be clear! It might even sentence you, based on the 'evidence' of your life.

But in Christ – you too will be truly, amazingly, eternally FREE!!

Thanks be to God and HALLELUYA!!

Reflections

How would the "evidence" of your life convict you as a Christ-follower?

What does "freedom" mean to you?

50

Identity Theft

Meanwhile, as Peter was sitting outside in the courtyard, a servant girl came over and said to him, **"You were one of those with Jesus the Galilean."**

But Peter denied it in front of everyone. **"I don't know what you are talking about,"** *he said.*

Later, out by the gate, another servant girl noticed him and said to those standing around, **"This man was with Jesus of Nazareth."**

Again Peter denied it, this time with an oath. **"I don't even know the man,"** *he said.*

A little later some other bystanders came over to him and said, **"You must be one of them;** *we can tell by your Galilean accent."*

Peter said, **"I swear by God, I don't know the man."** *And immediately the rooster crowed.*

Suddenly, Jesus' words flashed through Peter's mind: *"Before the rooster crows, you will deny me three times."* **And he went away, crying bitterly.**

-Matthew 26: 69-75 (New Living Translation)

All this time, Peter was sitting out in the courtyard. One servant girl came up to him and said, **"You were with Jesus the Galilean."**

In front of everyone there, he denied it. **"I don't know what you're talking about."**

As he moved over toward the gate, someone else said to the people there, **"This man was with Jesus the Nazarene."**

Again he denied it, salting his denial with an oath: **"I swear, I never laid eyes on the man."**

Shortly after that, some bystanders approached Peter. **"You've got to be one of them. Your accent gives you away."**

Then he got really nervous and swore. **"I don't know the man!"**

Just then a rooster crowed. **Peter remembered what Jesus had said:** *"Before the rooster crows, you will deny me three times."* **He went out and cried and cried and cried.**

- Matthew 26: 69-75 (The Message Version)

* * * * * * * * *

"Will Jesus know me when I get there?" *Worry deepened the lines already etched on her face from decades of life as a farmer's wife. I must have seemed confused. After all,* **here was a woman I'd been told was a lifelong church member.** Samantha sang in the choir and had coordinated the annual church barbeque for many years. She and her family helped rebuild the church after the tornado destroyed it in '85! I'd heard all these wonderful stories, and many more, from friends and family as they gathered in the hospital intensive care waiting area.

Her voice interrupted my thoughts. A smile crossed her face, temporarily masking the wince of pain underneath. "I bet those kids of mine have been telling you stories, haven't they? Well, lying here in this bed all these months, I've been thinking. You know, **my best friend died last year**. She was the best quiltmaker for miles around - I bet the best in the whole state! **Do you know how many people I told about Mabel and her quilts? I'd bet hundreds."**

OK - so what does making quilts and Mabel have to do with Jesus? Maybe it was the meds. Folks like her with end stage cancer on strong pain relief drugs sometimes didn't quite hold a coherent conversation. But then.....

Betty started to chuckle. "I bet you don't get what I'm saying, do you? You know, I would have thought I was crazy too a few months ago!" She sighed and shifted her weight, her face suddenly gray with pain.

"Whew! I think I feel better. Anyway, Mabel's passing got me to thinking. **Was she a better friend to me than Jesus? I mean, in all my, well, let's say more than 90 years, I could probably count on my hands (wouldn't even need my toes!) the people I've shared Jesus with.** *Oh, I don't mean in that 'Bible in your face', 'do you know where you're going' kind of way. I just mean in an everyday sort of way. So* **if I've shared Mabel's quiltmaking gift with hundreds, why haven't I shared my Savior -the Greatest Gift ever - with many more than that?"**

Ah ha! NOW I was getting the Mabel-Jesus connection! Betty was on a roll, her sharp eyes taking in my growing understanding.

SO, will He even know me? *When I think back, if I were Him (good thing I'm not!), would I even recognize me at all? I've had so many opportunities, and I've let....something.....rob me of my identity as a real Christian. I mean,* **if I really truly AM one of Jesus' disciples, His followers, how have I lost so much of my Jesus-identity?"**

After visiting with Betty for a while, praying with her and her family, and assuring her that Jesus would indeed know her (the Shepherd certainly knows His sheep), **I began the long walk back to my office** on the other side of the hospital.

Thoughts and prayers echoed through my mind as I walked. **WOULD Jesus recognize me the same way I recognized Him so many times?** *How about all those opportunities I had to share my VERY best friend with others - and hadn't?*

Like Peter, I cried as occasion after occasion flashed across my mind. I didn't need to hear the rooster crow. Wow.

My identity was being stolen, time after time, and I didn't even recognize it for what it was: the most enormous kind of.....identity theft!

* * * * * * * * *

Jesus knew Peter's humanity. *He loved Peter dearly.*
He knows ours, and our fear too. And - get this - He loves us wholeheartedly too!

How COULD we deny even KNOWING Jesus?

How could this happen? *What do we allow to steal our identity as Jesus-followers?*
Why would we allow this?

The truth is, **many times we feel like Peter** did in the courtyard that day.

Many time we too **find it much easier to pretend we don't even know who Jesus is**, let alone claim Him as Lord and Savior.

What's your identity? Who are you? How much of your identity as a disciple of Jesus the Christ have you allowed to be stolen?

Are you a victim of.......identity theft? *Most of us are.*

It's time. *Time to reclaim our identity as Christians - those who are 'with Jesus'.*

WILL Jesus know you when you 'get there'?
Will YOU know JESUS?

Don't let another day go by. *Recover your Jesus-identity NOW!!*

Reflections

How do people lose their Christ-identity?

What threatens to steal our identity as Christ-followers?

How can we protect that identity?

51

Black & White

Very early in the morning, the leading priests and other leaders met again to discuss how to persuade the Roman government to sentence Jesus to death. Then they bound him and took him to Pilate, the Roman governor.

When Judas, who had betrayed him, realized that Jesus had been condemned to die, he was filled with remorse. So he took the thirty pieces of silver back to the leading priests and other leaders. "I have sinned," he declared, "for I have betrayed an innocent man." "What do we care?" they retorted. "That's your problem."

Then Judas threw the money onto the floor of the Temple and went out and hanged himself.

The leading priests picked up the money. "We can't put it in the Temple treasury," they said, "since it's against the law to accept money paid for murder." After some discussion they finally decided to buy the potter's field, and they made it into a cemetery for foreigners. That is why the field is still called the Field of Blood. This fulfilled the prophecy of Jeremiah that says, "They took the thirty pieces of silver — the price at which he was valued by the people of Israel — and purchased the potter's field, as the Lord directed."

- Matthew 27: 1-10 (New Living Translation)

* * * * * * * * * *

"Daddy, I thought these were BLACK and WHITE pictures. I think you did it wrong, 'cause there's more GRAY than anything else. Maybe you should dip them back in that wet stuff again. THEN would they be black and white?"

Dad smiled at his daughter. **Since Mom had left, it had been just the two of them.** With work, household stuff, and all that came with single parenting, Troy had felt overwhelmed. Then his neighbor suggested maybe it would help if he took up a hobby. So he ran down the list of 'hobbies' he could think of. Hmmm....hunting (nope, away from home, child care $$), fishing (nope, daughter Holly hated anything wet and slimy), woodworking (again no, power tools and a six year old child - definitely not).

Then it happened - one of those 'God-moments'. They'd been walking in the mall, having just bought her what seemed like the fifth pair of shoes in a year, when she abruptly stopped, captivated by the window display in the photography shop. "Wow, Daddy!" she'd exclaimed, fascinated glee lighting up her face, **"Could you teach me to make THOSE?"** He'd thought. Then he'd swallowed. Amazing. No way she could possibly know her great granddad (Troy's grandpa) had been an award-winning nature photographer. No way.

"Well, honey, **I've never really taken pictures before** - certainly not really cool ones like those..."

"But Da-a-a-ddy - you could LEARN. I learn new stuff in school every day." Her small brow wrinkled in concentration. "Hey, I know! We'll learn TOGETHER! Come on, let's go in there!" And with that, their father-daughter photography team was born.

Now, **two years later, they had a darkroom in the basement.** They were new to black and white photography, but when Holly saw some of her great grandfather's work (all in black and white), she just HAD to try it. So here they were, developing their first set of black and whites.

But how to explain the gray in the 'black and white' pictures? "Well, honey, there's just a lot of gray in 'black and white'," he began, then saw the look of confusion on her face. **"OK, like the other day when you saw Jenny getting ready to hit her little brother.** Remember that? You pushed her away and she fell down, right?" Holly nodded. Holly remembered feeling really bad because she really liked Jenny, and Jenny'd scraped her knees when she fell.

"It's sort of like that. **It was wrong to push Jenny. But if you hadn't**, then her little brother might have really been hurt, right? I mean he's only three, and she was ready to hit him hard, so what do you think might have happened then?"

Holly was thinking hard. "Well, **Daddy, she's a lot bigger, and she was real mad**, and, well, I think she'dhave been real sorry if she hurt little Chad, even if she does say she hates him sometimes, but I still felt bad..."

"Exactly. **It's sort of like all this gray in these pictures.** Some things are plain black or white, right or wrong. But a lot of things are just, well, sort of gray!"

"I get it! Jenny'ssmile sparkled and she gave a little jump of excitement. "That's why Jesus came!"

What? Troy thought. *Where did that come from?*

"You KNOW, Daddy, like in church. The preacher said those people a long time ago had rules. Lots of them. But they could never do all of them just right, so God sent Jesus to give us great big GRACE! Like THAT! **That gray stuff, well it's just full of Jesus!** I've decided - gray's good - we'll keep it!" Her face got really serious.

"You know what, Daddy?" He waited. He just HAD to hear the rest. "What, Holly?"

"I need Jesus. I need him real bad, cause without Him, I just can't figure out all that gray!"

Holly professed her faith in Jesus and was baptized that next Sunday. This is the story her dad told as he stood with her.

May you too find the incredible Grace of Jesus the Christ in all the 'gray' of your life.

Reflections

How does Jesus help us "figure out all the gray" in our lives?

What do you think Holly meant when she said, "That gray stuff, well it's just full of Jesus"?

52

Are YOU a CHRISTIAN?

*Now Jesus stood before the governor; and the governor asked him, **"Are you the King of the Jews?" Jesus said, "You say so."*** *But when he was accused by the chief priests and elders, he did not answer.*
*Then **Pilate said to him, "Do you not hear** how many accusations they make against you?"*
*But he gave him no answer, not even to a single charge, so that **the governor was greatly amazed.***
- Matthew 27:11-14 (New Living Translation)

*Jesus was placed before the governor, who questioned him: **"Are you the King of the Jews?"***
Jesus said, "If you say so." *But when the accusations rained down hot and heavy from the high priests and religious leaders, he said nothing.*
Pilate asked him, "Do you hear *that long list of accusations? Aren't you going to say something?" Jesus kept silence – not a word from his mouth.*
*The **governor was impressed – really impressed.***
- Matthew 27: 11-14 (The Message Version)

* * * * * * * * *

It was an **intriguing sermon. Several of the youth had conducted an experiment** among their 'Christian' friends. **The question: How would you pick a Christian out of a crowd?** I mean, would they be different? Their discoveries were so surprising that they decided to share them in a sermon on Sunday morning.

They called it (are you ready?).......'Christians' Court' (after the popular 'People's Court' TV show).

Here are some **excerpts from the testimony** of several people accused of being 'Christ-followers'.

<u>Case #101</u>
   Bailiff: Your Honor, here we have Joe Smith.
   The charges: following that revolutionary, Jesus, a.k.a.'The Christ'

Judge: How do you plead, Mr. Smith?

156

Joe: Who, me? Your Honor, I was just standing on the corner when these, thesehuge guys came and shoved me in a big van. I mean, all I did was help some old dude push his car out of the street.

Judge: (clearing throat for effect) Mmm hmm. **How do you plead, then?**

(silence)

Prosecutor: Your Honor, let's let his actions speak for themselves. Exhibit #1 shows his attendance record at those 'Christian' meetings. Almost every week he shows up there.

Judge: Well, I'll take your silence, Mr. Smith, as a 'not guilty' plea. Continue, Mr. Prosecutor.

Prosecutor: Yes sir. Well, so these Christ-followers, they go around helping all sorts of people. It's their thing, you know? So he's obviously guilty!

Judge: Mr. Smith, I don't see an attorney with you. Would you like me to appoint one for you? These are serious charges, you know.

Joe: Nope. I'm fine here, really. Like I said before, I was just standing on the corner when thesehuge guys came and shoved me in a big van. I mean, all I did was help some old dude push his car out of the street.

Judge: I think we can clear this up quickly. **So Joe, ARE you a Christ-follower?**

Joe: Well, I go to church....I guess I am.

Judge: What happened after you helped the man with his car? Did you talk to him or anything?

Joe: Well, he did thank me. Oh, and he asked me why I missed my bus to help him. You see, my bus came while I was helping him.

Judge: And....

Joe: And I told him it was no big deal, and to have a nice day.

Prosecutor: Your Honor, really, the evidence is clear. He hangs out with those notorious Christ-followers, and here we have him missing his bus to work to help some guy he doesn't even know. **He's guilty for sure!**

Judge: Well, **I don't quite see it that way.** From what I've seen, a real Christ-follower would have taken the opportunity this man presented to talk about how this Christ had changed himm. He would at least have said something about how his faith called him to help those in need......and I see no record of him giving any money or helping with any of their work in the community. No evidence that he really even lets himself be seen with any of the known Christ-followers. **Dismissed! Next case?**

Prosecutor: But, Your Honor...?

Judge: I said DISMISSED! Mr. Smith, you're free to go.

Joe: Thank you, Your Honor, I knew if you heard the facts, you'd know I was innocent! Have a nice day!

* * * * * * * * *

<u>Case #102</u>

Bailiff: Your Honor, here we have Letiqua Johnson. The charges: following that revolutionary, Jesus, a.k.a.'The Christ'

Judge: How do you plead, Ms. Johnson?

Letiqua: Why, Your Honor, **I plead.....guilty!**

Judge: Mmmm hmmm. Well, let's hear the evidence. I've learned to be careful with these 'Christ-follower' cases. Too many appeals. Ms. Prosecutor?

Prosecutor: Oh, yes, evidence? Well, she too attends one of those 'Christ-Follower' gatherings quite regularly.

Judge: Just like our previous defendant? I certainly hope your evidence is stronger in this case. You wasted the court's time with that one! **I'm listening.**

Prosecutor: Well, she advertises her allegiance clearly! Here are just a few of our video clips (we have hundreds). Please direct your attention to the screen.

Judge: I'm looking.

Letiqua: There I am, there I am! I'm the one in the blue outfit!

Prosecutor: Like I said, **here she is holding up a big sign** - see what it says? 'Be happy, follow Christ!' That's her, winking and smiling at the camera - no doubt about it. Here's another clip. That's her, waving at the camera.....

Letiqua: Right there, Your Honor, in the jeans and cool t-shirt. See, it's got Jesus' picture, right on the front!

Judge: I see it. So is this it? A bunch of pictures of the defendant waving signs and wearing clothing with this Jesus' picture? Has she said anything, done anything that shows she's actually a Christ-FOLLOWER?

Letiqua: But Your Honor, you can tell I'm guilty. Just look at the pictures! Oh, here, I even have a cross in my purse somewhere. Just a minute (starts digging in her purse). Hang on....

Judge: Ms. Johnson. Ms. <u>Johnson</u>!

Letiqua: (flustered) Yes sir?

Judge: Let's say you found that cross of yours. What would you do with it? I mean, would you show it to me?

Letiqua: (nods yes)

Judge: All right. **Then what?**

Letiqua: What do you mean, then what?

Judge: What I mean, young lady, is **what would you tell me about it? Why do you carry it? What's it all about?**

Letiqua: Oh, thank God. **Here it is!** (She pulls a BIG cross out of the bottom of her purse.) Look, isn't it pretty? **It's gold, you know, and isn't it cool-looking?** Look at the pretty stones around the edges....and the one in the middle, do you know what that one is? It's a real ruby!

Prosecutor: Please, Your Honor, **she said she was guilty!**

Judge: I'll see that for myself, thank you. **I'm not so sure about that.** Ms. Johnson, is that all, I mean, is there anything else you'd like to tell me about that cross? Anything at all?

Letiqua: Ummm....I'm confused. **Don't you like it? Here, I'll put on.** It really does look great with this purple shirt I'm wearing, don't you think?

Judge: This is no REAL Christ-follower.Dismissed! You're free to leave, Ms. Johnson. Andyou, Ms. Prosecutor?

Prosecutor: Yes, Your Honor?

Judge: Next time you come in here, you'd better have a REAL Christ-follower to show me.

Prosecutor: But sir, do you know how hard they are to find these days?

* * * * * * * * *

So I share with yousome questions I often ask myself:
ARE you a Christian?
Could YOU be convicted of being a Christ-follower?
What would the evidence be? Would it be strong enough to convict you?

Court's in session - How do you plead?

Really?

Reflections

What would a "real" Christ-follower look like? Act like? How would you recognize one?

Would others recognize you as a disciple of Christ? How easy would it be to "convict" you?

53

In the Mob of Life

Now it was the governor's custom to release one prisoner to the crowd each year during the Passover celebration —anyone they wanted. This year there was a notorious criminal in prison, a man named Barabbas.

As **the crowds gathered before Pilate's house** that morning, he asked them, "Which one do you want me to release to you — Barabbas, or Jesus who is called the Messiah?" (He knew very well that the Jewish leaders had arrested Jesus out of envy.)

Just then, as Pilate was sitting on the judgment seat, his wife sent him this message: "Leave that innocent man alone, because I had a terrible nightmare about him last night."

Meanwhile, the **leading priests and other leaders persuaded the crowds** to ask for Barabbas to be released and for Jesus to be put to death. So when the governor asked again, "Which of these two do you want me to release to you?" **the crowd shouted back their reply: "Barabbas!"**

"But if I release Barabbas," Pilate asked them, "what should I do with Jesus who is called the Messiah?" And **they all shouted, "Crucify him!"**

"Why?" Pilate demanded. "What crime has he committed?" But **the crowd only roared the louder, "Crucify him!"**

Pilate saw that he wasn't getting anywhere and that a riot was developing. So he sent for a bowl of water and washed his hands before the crowd, saying, "I am innocent of the blood of this man. The responsibility is yours!" And **all the people yelled back, "We will take responsibility for his death— we and our children!"**

So Pilate released Barabbas to them. He ordered Jesus flogged with a lead-tipped whip, then turned him over to the Roman soldiers to crucify him.

- Matthew 27: 15-26 (New Living Translation)

* * * * * * * * * *

Picture this imaginary scene:

"Hey, Mom, who's Barabbas?"

"I don't know, honey, but he's sure safer to have on the loose than that Jesus. Look how much trouble follows HIM around! We don't need that kind of trouble. No, we're much safer with Barabbas than with Jesus on the loose!"

"Oh, but Mom.....?"

"What now, honey?"

"Well, **what if what they're saying about Jesus is true? I mean, what if he really IS the Messiah?**"

"Then it won't really matter, because he'll save himself. That's what the priests said earlier. Now SHHH! I can't hear a thing!"

"Mom! They're going to hurt Jesus. They're going to hurt him real bad! Are they really going to kill him, really? That's not right! What did he ever do to them, besides try to get them to listen to the truth?"

"Be QUIET! If someone hears you talking that nonsense, they'll think we're his followers! Like I said, we're safer with Barabbas. Jesus is trouble - big trouble. Now we'd better get home. Your father and brothers will be home soon and we need to fix supper."

* * * * * * * * * *

So, is Barabbas loose in your life..... or is Jesus?

Scripture tells us that we are to liveIN the world, but not be OF the world.

"Don't copy the behavior and customs of this world, but let God transform you into a new person by changing the way you think. Then you will know what God wants you to do, and you will know how good and pleasing and perfect his will really is." (Romans 12:2, New Living Translation)

You might have thought as you read the story of the mom and daughter above, *'How could she say that? Doesn't she know?'*

The truth is, we 'release Barabbas' quite often! And yes, we send Jesus off – to wherever – just as often too.

Part of our lives as disciples of Christ is taking an honest look at those times and bringing them to God in prayer, asking God to transform us, to change the way we think and act.

The mom is the story is acting in the way of her world – in many ways the same world we live in. Her daughter is preaching a fine sermon. Maybe she heard. Maybe.

God used that little girl in a mighty big way.
God can use you and I that way too!

So –who will be 'on the loose' in your life today?
Will it be Barabbas?
....or Jesus?

Reflections

How DO we "release Barabbas" in our lives?

How DO we "release Jesus" in our lives?

Name a concrete way we can "release Jesus".

54

Just One of the Crowd

*Then the soldiers of the governor took Jesus into the governor's headquarters, and **they gathered** the whole cohort around him.**They stripped him** and put a scarlet robe on him, and after twisting some thorns into a crown, **they put** it on his head. **They put** a reed in his right hand and knelt before him and mocked him, saying, "Hail, King of the Jews!"**They spat** on him, and took the reed and struck him on the head. After mocking him, **they stripped him** of the robe and put his own clothes on him. Then **they led him away** to crucify him.*

- Matthew 27: 27-31 (New Revised Standard Version)

*Some of the governor's soldiers took Jesus into their headquarters and called out the entire battalion.**They stripped him** and put a scarlet robe on him.**They made** a crown of long, sharp thorns and put it on his head, and **they placed** a stick in his right hand as a scepter. Then **they knelt** before him in mockery, yelling, "Hail! King of the Jews!"And **they spit** on him and grabbed the stick and beat him on the head with it.When **they** were finally tired of mocking him, **they** took off the robe and put his own clothes on him again. Then **they led him away** to be crucified.*

- Matthew 27: 27-31 (New Living Translation)

*The soldiers assigned to the governor took Jesus into the governor's palace and got the entire brigade together for some fun. **They stripped him** and dressed him in a red toga. **They plaited** a crown from branches of a thorn bush and set it on his head. **They put** a stick in his right hand for a scepter. Then **they knelt** before him in mocking reverence: "Bravo! King of the Jews!" **they said**. "bravo!" Then **they spit** on him and hit him on the head with the stick. When **they** had had their fun, **they** took off the toga and put his own clothes back on him. Then **they proceeded out to the crucifixion.***

- Matthew 27: 27-31 (The Message Version)

* * * * * * * * * *

"But, I didn't DO anything! I was just there - it was those other guys that beat him up and all. Really, it's not fair! I didn't DO anything!"

"Well, here we have video, Justin, courtesy of Channel 2News, of you...**this IS you, right? Smiling while this other guy is telling your buddies to 'get him good'?"**

"But Dad, I didn't DO anything!"

"Son, stop, OK? If I hear you say that one more time, I think I'll....I'll just throw up! Understand?"

"But Dad!"

"Here's your reality check, son. You did nothing. Nothing at all. You didn't try to stop it. You said nothing. You didn't go for help. So yes, you did do 'something'. You're one of that crowd, and they're - every one of them, including you - **guilty as sin. No, I take that back - you're guilty OF sin."**

* * * * * * * * *

Did you notice all the 'theys' in this Scripture?

How many of us have been 'one of the crowd'?
Ever seen something you know is wrong, something Jesus would NEVER have stood for, and there you.... stood?
OK, here's the truth: **all of us have. That's right - ALL of us.**

Can you see him? He's in the back of the brigade of soldiers that day in Jerusalem. **Just one of the guys.** He didn't say anything, didn't mock Jesus himself, and certainly didn't hit him - himself, that is.

But like the saying goes, **'If you don't stand for something, you'll fall for anything'.** Our soldier in the back did, and we do too.

Can you hear Jesus say, **"Forgive them, Father, they don't know what they're doing?"** (Luke 23:34, New Living Translation) He says that to us today just as surely as He said it that long ago day on Calvary.

Most times, we really don't know the full picture of what we really ARE doing as 'one of the crowd', any more than that soldier in the back of the brigade or many in the crowds yelling for Jesus to be crucified.

Go back and **read the dad's last response to his son again:**

"Here's your reality check, son. You did nothing. Nothing at all. You didn't try to stop it. You said nothing. You didn't go for help. So yes, you did do 'something'. You're one of that crowd, and they're - every one of them, including you - guilty as sin. No, I take that back - you're guilty OF sin."

Hear God's voice in that dad's - calling us, His sons and daughters, to take an honest look at how we live our lives. **Which crowd are we part of?**

Reflections

What does this saying mean to you: "If you don't stand for anything, you'll fall for anything."?

How did you react when you read the dad's response to his son: "Here's your reality check, son. You did nothing. Nothing at all. You didn't try to stop it. You said nothing. You didn't go for help. So yes, you did do 'something'. You're one of that crowd, and they're - every one of them, including you - guilty as sin. No, I take that back - you're guilty OF sin."?

Which crowd are you a part of most times? How does that need to change (or does it)?

55

What About Simon?

After mocking him, they stripped him of the robe and put his own clothes on him. Then they led him away to crucify him. As they went out, they came upon a man from Cyrene named Simon; they compelled this man to carry his cross. And when they came to a place called Golgotha (which means Place of a Skull), they offered him wine to drink, mixed with gall; but when he tasted it, he would not drink it. And when they had crucified him, they divided his clothes among themselves by casting lots; then they sat down there and kept watch over him. Over his head they put the charge against him, which read, "This is Jesus, the King of the Jews." Then two bandits were crucified with him, one on his right and one on his left. Those who passed by derided him, shaking their heads and saying, "You who would destroy the temple and build it in three days, save yourself! If you are the Son of God, come down from the cross." In the same way the chief priests also, along with the scribes and elders, were mocking him, saying, "He saved others; he cannot save himself. He is the King of Israel; let him come down from the cross now, and we will believe in him. He trusts in God; let God deliver him now, if he wants to; for he said, 'I am God's Son.'" The bandits who were crucified with him also taunted him in the same way.

- Matthew 27: 37-44 (New Revised Standard Version)

When they had had their fun, they took off the toga and put his own clothes back on him. Then they proceeded out to the crucifixion. Along the way they came on a man named Simon and made him carry Jesus' cross. Arriving at Golgotha, the place they call "Skull Hill", they offered him a mild painkiller (a mixture of wine and myrrh), but when he tasted it he wouldn't drink it.

After they had finished nailing him to the cross and were waiting for him to die, they whiled away the time by throwing dice for his clothes. Above his head they had posted the criminal charge against him: THIS IS JESUS, THE KING OF THE JEWS.

Along with him, they also crucified two criminals, one to his right, the other to his left. People passing along the road jeered, shaking their heads in mock lament: "You bragged that you could tear down the Temple and then rebuild it in three days - so show us your stuff! Save yourself! If you're really God's Son, come down from that cross!" The high priests, along with the religious scholars and leaders, were right there mixing it up with the rest of them, having a great time poking fun at him: "He saved others - he can't save himself! King of Israel, is he? Then let him get down from that cross. We'll ALL become believers then! He was so sure of God - well, let him rescue his 'Son' now - if he wants him! He did claim to be God's Son, didn't he? Even the two criminals crucified next to him joined in the mockery.

- Matthew 28: 31-44 (The Message Version)

* * * * * * * * *

166

"It's just a small part. Can't you help me out, just this once?" Walt, the youth leader, was really in a pinch. Three weeks till the play, and short this one part.... The hope was clear in his eyes as he faced his son.

"Well, you know I haven't been to church in a while, but..." Todd could feel his feet itching - itching to be anywhere else. What was his dad thinking? He hadn't been to church in, well,...

"It's a really small part, and you have been working out. You look really good, by the way." OK, now Walt knew he was begging, but...

"Thanks, Dad. Wrestling team'll do that for you, you know."

"Well, I need someone to play Simon in the play we're doing about the last days of Jesus. All you have to do is be strong and carry the crossbeam - the big wooden one - down the church aisle. Then you're done!" Maybe Todd would help out if it was a small part...?

"That's it? Well, then what do I do once I get up there with the cross? Just stand there, like a dummy, or what?" Todd laughed. "You know Dad, I'm a little big to just disappear!"

At 6 foot 5, Todd WAS a little big to disappear. Hmmm. Walt looked again at the script. Sure enough, it did look like Simon just 'disappeared'! It got him to thinking. What DID happen to Simon, anyway?

Later that evening, Todd came out to the garage to talk. Walt could tell his son had been really thinking. "Dad? It's about that Simon thing at church. Still want me to help out?"

Walt knew his son well enough to know there was a 'rest of the story' here, so he simply nodded, put his screwdriver down, and turned his full attention on Todd.

"Well, Dad, here's the thing. I don't think that Simon guy disappeared. I mean, really, who'd miss all that action? Don't you think he'd want to stick around to see what happened next? I'll take the part.....if you let me REALLY play Simon. How about it?"

That began some wonderful father-son conversations about all the 'Simons' they'd known.

There was the missionary who'd 'carried the cross' for World Vision in Bangladesh. Walt remembered him speaking at their church a few years back. Recently he'd heard the guy - Steve, maybe? - wasn't even involved in church any more. Todd talked about a young lady, Maria, in his class who'd stood up for a deaf classmate, really 'walking the extra mile' for her. Lately, though, it seemed Maria just ignored the mean-spirited teasing directed at her one-time buddy. Maria sure had dropped the cross on that one.

Walt decided to trust his son with the part - the whole part. When rehearsal time came, Todd's ideas and performance simply blew him away. 'Simon' carried the cross well, and then, well, then he hung around the fringes. He saw it all: the nailing of Jesus to the cross, the posting of the sign above His head, the mocking, jeering crowds, all of it.

As Todd became Simon, he lived out his own struggles about following Jesus. In doing so, he demonstrated the reality of truly living as one who answers the call of Jesus: "If any of you wants to be my follower," he told them, "you must put aside your selfish ambition, shoulder your cross, and follow me." (Mark 8:34, New Living Translation)

When asked by a friend about his performance later, Todd said, "I don't think it was a one-time thing for Simon. I think he kept carrying that cross for the rest of his life. I think that's what Jesus meant. Not just when it's convenient, or when we're forced to do it, like the Bible says happened to Simon that day. Nope, He means every day. Simon's life changed that day, and mine's changed after putting myself in his shoes too. And to think, I almost told my dad 'no way'!"

As Todd turned to leave, his friend saw the back of Todd's shirt and smiled. "Ask me about Simon!", it said, in bold neon green. Oh, yeah. Todd had changed all right!

* * * * * * * * * *

So what happens to us after our initial encounter with Jesus, our first realization that following Him really can change our lives? Do we just 'disappear' into the crowd, back into our lives the way they were before we heard about Him?

Or do we, like Todd portrayed Simon of Cyrene, 'hang around the edges' of a life of faith for a while, waiting and watching, before we once more 'pick up the cross' to follow Jesus?

You know, there's nothing wrong with 'hanging around the edges' if we're growing and being equipped to be good, strong cross-carriers'! We'll find ourselves growing and being transformed by God's grace and the moving of the Holy Spirit. Before we know it, we'll be truly traveling through life with hearts and lives full of the Good News of Christ Jesus! Before we know it, we'll be God's instruments, connecting others to the amazing, grace-filled, cross-carrying life with Jesus the Christ!

So, what ABOUT Simon?

What about US?

Reflections

How could someone be growing and transforming as they "hang around the edges" of a faith life?

Why are we tempted to "disappear into the crowd" instead of living cross-carrying lives?

56

The Miracle of Hope

*From noon on, **darkness came over the whole land** until three in the afternoon. And about three o'clock Jesus cried with a loud voice, "Eli, Eli, lema sabachthani?" that is, **"My God, my God, why have you forsaken me?"***

When some of the bystanders heard it, they said, "This man is calling for Elijah."

At once one of them ran and got a sponge, filled it with sour wine, put it on a stick, and gave it to him to drink. But the others said, "Wait, let us see whether Elijah will come to save him."

*Then **Jesus cried again with a loud voice and breathed his last.***

*At that moment the **curtain of the temple was torn in two, from top to bottom. The earth shook, and the rocks were split. The tombs also were opened**, and many bodies of the saints who had fallen asleep were raised. After his resurrection they came out of the tombs and entered the holy city and appeared to many.*

*Now when the centurion and those with him, who were keeping watch over Jesus, saw the earthquake and what took place, they were terrified and said, **"Truly this man was God's Son!"***

***Many women were also there, looking on from a distance**; they had followed Jesus from Galilee and had provided for him. Among them were Mary Magdalene, and Mary the mother of James and Joseph, and the mother of the sons of Zebedee.*

- Matthew 27: 45-56 (New Revised Standard Version)

*From noon to three, **the whole earth was dark.** Around mid-afternoon Jesus groaned out of the depths, crying loudly, "Eli, Eli, lama sabachthani?" which means, **"My God, My God, why have you abandoned me?"***

Some bystanders who heard him said, "He's calling for Elijah."

One of them ran and got a sponge soaked in sour wine and lifted it on a stick so he could drink. The others joked, "Don't be in such a hurry. Let's see if Elijah comes and saves him."

*But **Jesus, again crying loudly, breathed his last.***

*At that moment, the **Temple curtain was ripped in two, top to bottom. There was an earthquake, and rocks were split in pieces. What's more, tombs were opened up**, and many bodies of believers asleep in their graves were raised. (After Jesus' resurrection, they left the tombs, entered the holy city, and appeared to many.)*

*The captain of the guard and those with him, when they saw the earthquake and everything else that was happening, were scared to death. They said, **"This has to be the Son of God!"***

***There were also quite a few women watching from a distance**, women who had followed Jesus from Galilee in order to serve him. Among them were Mary Magdalene, Mary the mother of James and Joseph, and the mother of the Zebedee brothers.*

- Matthew 27: 45-56 (The Message Version)

* * * * * * * * * *

"Sir? Sir?" **The fire investigator's voice interrupted Carl's helpless, hopeless thoughts.** The call had come in the middle of the night. By the time the fire department had reached the church, the building's shell was all that remained standing.

"Sir?" Carl looked up at the inspector's third try. "Yes? Sorry. I just..." A single tear escaped the corner of Carl's eye.

"Well sir,...I've got good news and then...other news."
"It's Carl. Just Carl. And I'll take the good news first. Lord knows I can use some of that right about now."

"OK then, **good news it is. It's not arson."**
Well, if that's all the good news,... Carl thought. He planted his feet firmly on the ground for the bad news.

"Well...Carl...**the bad news is that someone did start the fire here.** Looks like some homeless person was camped out in the back. I found their campfire, all their stuff too, looks like anyway. Seems you both got something in common. Sorry about that. Might give you some trouble getting the insurance company to pay too. Let's see....." He looked down at his clipboard, noticed the name of the church's insurance company and groaned.

Carl was really worried now. Insurance money was the only way he figured they could ever rebuild. Great - more bad news.

"Well, here's the thing with this company. **I bet the price was cheap, wasn't it?** No need to answer that. Anyway, I can almost bet they're **going to say you should have put up some kind of barriers to keep these folks out.** They'll say then this probably wouldn't have happened..."

Carl was shocked. "You mean they'd want us to put up big gates or something to keep people OUT?" **The local homeless shelter was their main ministry.** Why, a fourth of their congregation came from there!

So the church began meeting and worshipping in the local elementary school.

Sure enough, when Carl contacted the insurance company, **that's exactly what the insurance adjustor said when he saw the fire department report.** They wouldn't be getting much money there. And they soon found out the **school wasn't too keen** on having the folks from the shelter in there either.

It was several weeks before Carl could make himself go back by the old church, and what he saw when he did simply amazed him. The lot was cleared, and that wasn't all - there was a big tent pitched smack in the middle of the lot! **A hand-lettered sign propped outside read, "Miracle of Hope Christian Church - Disciples Born and Raised Here!"**

Miracle of Hope Christian Church. Carl got out of his car and walked slowly over the charred ground, past where the rose garden once stood, past the burned-out playground, and finally stood in front of the sign.

"Can I help you, sonny?" A crackly old-timer's voice called from inside the tent. "Don't just stand out there - come on in!" A face peeked out of the tent. Mabel! "Why Carl, we wondered if we'd ever see you again! Like what we've done so far? **Come see the garden!"**

"Garden? In the middle of all this - a garden?" The words popped out of his mouth before he could hold them back. Mabel started laughing. Soon they were both laughing as she walked him around back of the tent. "Yep, remember that community garden we were going to start? Well, here it is!" It was indeed. The soil had been dug and neat rows of plants were poking their heads out of the soil.

"You know, Carl, this soil will be better now. All that burned stuff - it's good for it. Well, just so's you know, over there we'll have the new sanctuary, and right there, why that'll be the nursery. Back here we'll have the new food pantry and we figure a nice kitchen to wash all the great veggies from that garden!"

Oh boy. **How was he going to tell her there's be no money** *from the insurance company for rebuilding?* "Well, Mabel, the insurance, well, they said...."

She interrupted him mid-sentence. **"Oh, honey, I know.** I met that awful man right after the fire. **And you know what? We're GOING to rebuild this church.** Yes sirree. Right now, over at the shelter, know who's there? Why we have a carpenter and a cement man. They're veterans too. A bit down on their luck right now, but I've got 'em goin'. **We've all been coming over here** to work and worship every day since the fire. Any of the folks meeting at the school want to help?"

Six months later, the food pantry opened. A month later, the sanctuary was ready, and soon after that the kitchen was getting full-time use as produce flowed through from the community garden out back.

Miracle of Hope Christian Church was born on a crisp clear Sunday morning in November. As Carl stood on the same spot where he'd cried for the loss of the church, he now stood crying again – but this time tears of joy streamed down his face.

* * * * * * * * *

Any burned out places in your life? The disciples have been there. The women who watched Jesus the Messiah, their heavenly Hope, die a horrible death – they've been there too.

They cried the same tears Carl cried the day of the fire. **Like Carl, you and I have been there** in various ways (or we will be at some time). Helpless. Hopeless.

Impossible as it may seem, Jesus waits with your miracle of hope. He waits to plant new seeds, to raise new possibilities, new opportunities, and new life – in just those places where it looks the least likely!

Why is this?
Because, in the words of the guard, *"This has to be the Son of God!"*

Amen then, amen for Carl, and AMEN for you and I!

May Jesus the Christ plant Miracles of Hope in your life too

Reflections

Have you (or someone you know) had a "burned out place" in life? How did you (or they) get through it?

How is this church demonstrating its name, "Miracle of Hope Christian Church"?

How do you think it's living out its motto, "Disciples Born and Raised Here!"?

How does your church live this out? If you think it doesn't, how could it?

57

The Seal of Hope

*That evening a **rich disciple name Joseph from the town of Arimathea went and asked for Jesus' body.** Pilate gave orders for it to be given to Joseph, who took the body and wrapped it in a clean linen cloth. Then **Joseph put the body in his own tomb** that had been cut into solid rock and had never been used. **He rolled a big stone against the entrance to the tomb and went away.***

All this time Mary Magdalene and the other Mary were sitting across from the tomb.

*On the next day, which was a Sabbath, the **chief priests and the Pharisees** went together to Pilate. They said, "Sir, we remember what that liar said while he was still alive. He claimed that in three days he would come back from death. So **please order the tomb to be carefully guarded for three days. If you don't, his disciples may come and steal his body.** Then they will tell the people that he has been raised to life, and this last lie will be worse than the first one."*

Pilate said to them, "All right, take some of your soldiers and guard the tomb as well as you know how." So they sealed it tight and placed soldiers there to guard it.

- Matthew 27: 57-66 (Contemporary English Version)

*Late in the afternoon a **wealthy man from Arimathea, a disciple of Jesus, arrived.** His name was Joseph. He went to Pilate and **asked for Jesus' body.** Pilate granted his request. Joseph **took the body and wrapped it in clean linens, put it in his own tomb,** a new tomb only recently cut into the rock, **and rolled a large stone across the entrance.***

But Mary Magdalene and the other Mary stayed, sitting in plain view of the tomb.

*After sundown, the **high priests and Pharisees** arranged a meeting with Pilate. They said, "Sir, we just remembered that that liar announced while he was still alive, 'After three days I will be raised.' **We've got to get that tomb sealed until the third day. There's a good chance his disciples will come and steal the corpse** and then go around saying, 'He's risen from the dead.' Then we'll be worse off than before, the final deceit surpassing the first."*

Pilate told them, "You will have a guard. Go ahead and secure it the best you can." So they went out and secured the tomb, sealing the stone and posting guards.

- Matthew 27: 57-66 (The Message Version)

* * * * * * * * * *

"There was so much more he had to do. I just know it. No one should die so young."

His words broke into my prayers in the small hospital chapel. He caught my eye, nodded, sat down by me, and continued.

173

"They didn't have any place to bury him, not even any family to claim his body. My dad's going to give him his grave plot. But still, what about all the great things he could have done? **Where's the hope in that?"**

A few weeks later he came looking for me again. **"I had to tell you what happened after my buddy's funeral, after they buried him and all.",** he began. "I guess I didn't tell you the other night, but he was all set to go play triple-A ball. **He was going to be a star, I could tell.** He was that good. But you know, I was so busy paying attention to that, I never really got to know him. Knew him ten years and still..."

I invited him into the office and he told me more. "Yeah, we knew he didn't have any family, but **what we didn't know was who he really was.** I thought it all died when he did, but I was looking in all the wrong places. Incredible things are happening. Seems he inherited a bunch of money a long time ago when his family was killed in an accident, but he lived in an old apartment downtown! He put all that money into a foundation. We got a letter from the lawyer today telling us about it. Tutoring programs, a homeless shelter, an assisted living place...the list went on and on! All existing because **Will 'wanted to place as many seals of hope in the world as he could',** the lawyer said. I called to talk to this lawyer-guy. He knew Will's whole family, said he took his folks' death really hard. Then Will decided to 'do a Jesus-thing', he said. **He was determined that death should never be the end, said following Jesus meant 'rolling away as many stones as I can', as he put it once.** So he started the foundation, called it - are you ready? Stone-Rollers Anonymous! All the organizations on that list were pretty much out of hope when he discovered them. He got them back on their feet, every last one of them. Ten years I knew him, and I thought it was the baseball that gave him that bounce in his step."

"What now?" I asked him. He smiled. "**Oh, Will left me something.** Don't know how he found out my mom and us kids lived in a shelter once, but maybe that's why.....well, he left me the homeless shelter to run - how cool is that? **There were at least ten of us he left letters for, all closed with these really cool seals. Big stickers labeled "Seal of Hope".** The lawyer told us those seals were really important to Will. He read the will to us, then told us, 'If you break that Seal of Hope, you accept what Will's leaving for you.'"

"So how's it going?" I was really intrigued now, wishing I'd known Will myself. "Well," **he smiled, I'm busy 'rolling stones' and 'sealing hope' into people's lives!** And my dad (Joe) has decided that Joseph of Arimathea is his biblical mentor. You should see how he's changed! He's got a light in his life he hasn't had since we lost mom a few years back. I think, no, I **know that Will's 'Seals of Hope' will live on long after we're all gone.** Well, I've got to go - we're starting a clinic at the shelter and we've got some of the doctors and residents on board to help. Now I'm trying to get the hospital on board - pray for me, OK?"

* * * * * * * * *

Not the 'hope' Will's friend had in mind. Nope, he thought Will's hope lay in an awesome major league baseball career. **Truth was, Will's hope lay in a major-league hope career!**

Jesus was rarely what people expected. Even today, Jesus surprises people regularly. Then, they expected a completely different Messiah than what God sent. Their hope rested in a human definition of deliverance. Good thing God had an immensely bigger plan!

When Jesus' body was sealed in that tomb, **I wonder what the Marys were thinking** as they watched all this from their spot within view of the tomb. Was hope forever sealed in that tomb? What now?

And **Joseph of Arimathea – what about him?** Did he mourn the death of this Jesus, whom he had come to believe was truly the Son of God? Were all his hopes sealed in that tomb – his own tomb? What now?

We like to seal Jesus up too. Jesus is for Sundays, maybe also for when we gather with our 'church-friends', certainly not for every day! Well, maybe we unseal Him when we have tough decisions to make. It's like we take Jesus out when we need him and them seal Him up safely again. Then again, when we do 'let Him out', we're watching to see what happens (kind of like the Marys).

I wonder **what would happen if we truly let the full measure of Jesus' hope rule our lives?** I mean every day? How would our lives change if we lived fully in the hope of His resurrection? I mean, really, we DO KNOW the victory of God in this story – could we live each day like we believe it?

We have Christ's seal of hope on our lives the second we accept Him as our Lord and Savior. It's a seal made to be opened up and shared, not closed up and hidden. Remember Jesus words:
"No one would light a lamp and then cover it up or put it under a bed. No, lamps are mounted in the open, where they can be seen by those entering the house." (Luke 8:16, New Living Translation)

Remember who it was that wanted to be sure that tomb's seal was never broken?
Then remember that God's Way was to burst that seal forever!

Who do we follow? Who do we serve?
Break the seal! Release Christ's hope into and through your life – each and every day!

Reflections

How do we "seal Jesus up"?

Imagine you are one of "the Marys". How would that be? What would you be thinking as you watched?

What if you were Joseph of Arimathea?

How will people know we serve a RISEN Savior and Lord?

58

Afraid to Hope

After the Sabbath, as the first day of the week was dawning, Mary Magdalene and the other Mary went to see the tomb.

And suddenly there was a great earthquake; for an angel of the Lord, descending from heaven, came and rolled back the stone and sat on it.His appearance was like lightning, and his clothing white as snow.For fear of him the guards shook and became like dead men.

But *the angel said to the women, "Do not be afraid; I know that you are looking for Jesus who was crucified. He is not here; for he has been raised, as he said. Come, see the place where he lay.*Then go quickly and tell his disciples, 'He has been raised from the dead, and indeed he is going ahead of you to Galilee; there you will see him.' This is my message for you."

So *they left the tomb quickly with fear and great joy*, and ran to tell his disciples.

Suddenly Jesus met them and said, "Greetings!" And they came to him, took hold of his feet, and worshiped him.Then *Jesus said to them, "Do not be afraid;* go and tell my brothers to go to Galilee; there they will see me."

- Matthew 28: 1-10 (New Revised Standard Version)

After the Sabbath, as the first light of the new week dawned, Mary Magdalene and the other Mary came to keep vigil at the tomb. Suddenly the earth reeled and rocked under their feet as God's angel came down from heaven, came right up to where they were standing.

He rolled back the stone and then sat on it. Shafts of lightning blazed from him. His garments shimmered snow-white. They were so frightened, they couldn't move.

The **angel spoke to the women: "There is nothing to fear here. I know you're looking for Jesus, the One they nailed to the cross. He is not here. He was raised, just as he said. Come and look at the place where he was placed.**

"Now, get on your way quickly and tell his disciples, 'He is risen from the dead. He is going on ahead of you to Galilee. You will see him there.' That's the message.

The women, deep in wonder and full of joy, lost no time in leaving the tomb. They ran to tell the disciples. Then **Jesus met them, stopping them in their tracks.** "Good morning!" he said. They fell to their knees, embraced his feet, and worshipped him. Jesus said, "You're holding on to me for dear life! **Don't be frightened like that.** Go tell my brothers that they are to go to Galilee, and that I'll meet them there."

- Matthew 28: 1-10 (The Message Version)

176

* * * * * * * * *

"Jesus? For me? Yeah, right. Whatever."
That was how the conversation started. **This young woman, a pastor's daughter** as I soon discovered, had very firm, and very informed (or so it would seem) opinions about the whole 'religion thing', as she called it. **Her name was Holly.** She was a new server at the restaurant where I worked.

"You know that tomb, THE tomb, the one with Jesus in it? Well, He never came out of there in my life. Nope, He's sealed up, and that's it." We went on to talk about how a lot of people would probably identify with her point, and **I asked her why she thought those women went to the tomb that morning.** "Well, I know THAT,"Holly answered quickly, "They went there to take care of the body, you know, it was the 'women's' thing to do!"

Then **I asked her about the time Jesus died in her life.** "Well," she hesitated, "You're a pastor, right? Well, OK then." I could feel a test coming on.... **"Well, here's how it is.** Some guy just jumped out in front of my car on the highway and I hit him. He died."Holly waited. I waited.

"Well, you haven't left yet." She seemed surprised, so I told her I was waiting for the rest of the story. A glint of challenge shone in her eyes. **"OK then, I was devastated. I went to my church, you know the one my dad pastors?** Well, they told me it was pretty straight forward. I was a murderer. When people found out, they almost wouldn't even look at me. That's the day Jesus died for me."

Wow. I was still puzzled though, I mean the guy JUMPED in front of her car! So I challenged her. **"So, Jesus died. Have you been to the tomb?"**

"Have I been WHERE?" Holly's eyes heldthat 'you can't be serious' look. "Really, have you ever been back to where it happened? Ever wondered about that guy's family?"

Hollytold me his family had sent her a card, a really nice card. The man's mother wrote a wonderful letter with it too, about how her son Carl had lots of problems and had been kidding (they thought) about killing himself that very morning. **She wrote her address and phone number in the card in case Holly ever wanted to talk.**

"So," I asked, **"Did you ever call her?"**
"I was afraid to. I mean, I wanted her to forgive me, as you said, I wanted to see Jesus in all this, you know, out of that tomb and everything. But.....**I was afraid to hope too much."**
"I wonder if she's still at that address. How long has it been?"
Holly thought a minute. "It seems like forever, but it's just been nine months."

We talked a while and Holly left. I could tell she was thinking about our conversation as she went out the door.

We worked different shifts, so I didn't see her for a few days. **Then one evening she came in** with a friend. **"I want you to meet Rosa,"** she began. "You know that Jesus-in-the-tomb thing you asked me about? Well, I finally called her. **Rosa is the mother I told you about."** Rosa interrupted, reaching out and enveloping me in a huge hug. "We've been so worried about this little girl." she said, patting Holly on the shoulder, **"We've been praying for her ever since our Carl was killed, praying that God would touch her and heal her, praying that Jesus would be right with her holding her tight."**

Then Holly surprised me. "Rosa took me there. To where it happened, and to Carl's grave. And you know what? **She told that same story you did the other day - the one about the women and the tomb.** I could almost feel the earth shake as Rosa told me about their prayers for me. And you know what else? **Jesus is DEFINITELY out of the tomb for me.** I'm going to Rosa's church - and I've even invited my father." She laughed. "I don't think he'll come, but...."

Rosa laughed. "Afraid to hope, are we?" She pointed at me. "I think your new friend's right. Your father needs to let Jesus out of that tomb - he needs to find that Living Jesus!"

* * * * * * * * *

Are you ever afraid to hope? We all have our times, don't we?
Take a look at your life today. Are you living as if Jesus is still in that tomb? (Psst! - Let Him out!)
Would others be able to tell that you serve a RISEN Savior?

The women who came to the tomb that day had weathered the storms of the previous days together. They too **were afraid to hope.** Then Hope appeared, bigger and brighter than they had ever imagined, and they were afraid again!
So it is with us.

Both the angel and Jesus told them not to be afraid. Hope - alive before their very eyes!

Their lives were never the same - they'd met the risen Savior, and He literally lit up their lives.
He'll do the same for us.....if we'll let Him.

Will we? (Psst! ... Let him out!!)

Reflections

What would you say to Holly's dad?

What would make someone afraid to hope too much?

What would you say to that person?

59

Hope on the Way

While they were going, **some of the guard went into the city and told the chief priests** *everything that had happened.*

After the priests had assembled with the elders, **they devised a plan** *to give a large sum of money to the soldiers,telling them,* **"You must say, 'His disciples came by night and stole him** *away while we were asleep.'If this comes to the governor's ears, we will satisfy him and keep you out of trouble."*

So they took the money and did as they were directed. *And this story is still told among the Jews to this day.*
- Matthew 28: 11-15 (New Revised Standard Version)

As the women were on their way into the city, **some of the men who had been guarding the tomb went to the leading priests and told them** *what had happened.*

A meeting of all the religious leaders was called, and **they decided to bribe the soldiers.** *They told the soldiers,* **"You must say, 'Jesus' disciples came during the night while we were sleeping, and they stole his body.'** *If the governor hears about it, we'll stand up for you and everything will be all right."*

So **the guards accepted the bribe and said what they were told to say.** *Their story spread widely among the Jews, and they still tell it today.*
- Matthew 28: 11-15 (New Living Translation)

Meanwhile, the **guards had scattered, but a few of them went into the city and told the high priests** *everything that had happened.*

They called a meeting of the religious leaders and **came up with a plan:** *They took a large sum of money and gave it to the soldiers, bribing them to say,* **"His disciples came in the night and stole the body** *while we were sleeping." They assured them, "If the governor hears about your sleeping on duty, we will make sure you don't get blamed."*

The soldiers took the bribe and did as they were told. *That story, cooked up in the Jewish High Council, is still going around.*
- Matthew 28: 11-15 (The Message Version)

* * * * * * * * * *

Jared was frozen in place in the middle of the swirling, chaotic crowd. **Yelling, screaming, crying, and flying trash filled the air** of the New York Stock Exchange trading floor that day. He sunk into the nearest chair

179

as he witnessed the **stock market crash**. The orders had really flown in the last day. Options, options, and more options - it seemed that's all his clients had been doing. **Options to buy, options to sell, on and on......**

Jared looked around him at familiar faces, many now almost unrecognizable in the face of catastrophe. *What was it his wife Penny had said just a few hours ago as he left home?* Oh yes, something he hadn't remembered her ever saying before. "I've been praying a lot lately," she'd begun, reaching up to tilt hissix foot four head down to her five foot two gaze. **"I'm praying for both of us today, because I think we've lost our way. I** mean, is this all? Is this all?" She waved her hand around their beautiful living room. **"You talk so much about options** - so are we exercising our 'God-options', because I just don't know any more...."

Too late.He could see it allaround him. **Too late - or was it?** As Jared sat in the middle of what seemed like absolute disaster, the Presence of God washed through him. Why hadn't he seen it before? **In those chaotic moments, God's truth in Christ met his crashing life.** Penny was right. Jared sat with his head in his hands in prayer as his life's 'options' raced through his mind - and heart. Time and time again he realized **he'd chosen his own options instead of God's. Over and over.**

It was like God was (amazingly) showing him BOTH his mistaken choices AND incredible hope. **He still had options to choose!** Knowing that his friends and colleagues probably thought he was crazy (or had some great inside information - which in a sense he did), he left the trading floor that day with a smile on his face and hope in his heart.

"So, how are you, honey? I've been watching the news...." **Concern etched Penny's face as he walked through their front door.** Then she looked - really looked - at her husband of fifteen years. **Who WAS this man? He looked, well, he looked.....almost HAPPY!**

* * * * * * * * *

"My new dad tells me he finally 'exercised God's options'....and that's how me and my two brothers found a family - a real mom and dad!"Twelve year old Sean sat back down to a chorus of 'Cool' and 'Awesome' from his new classmates. They'd been asked to share how they'd spent their summers, and Sean had been the last to speak. **He and his two brothers had given up hope of ever finding a real family,** but the chaplain at the group home kept telling them that no matter what they should always try to do what God was leading them to do.

So the brothers had kept on choosing for Christ the best they knew. Like the women in this Scripture who kept on walking where Jesus sent them - even when trouble brewed around them, **even when no one else seemed to 'get it', these boys kept on walking in Jesus' Way.**

Jared and Penny were amazingly blessed by their three new sons. As they stood in church to testify to this amazing miracle in their lives, many who heard were challenged to really look at the 'options' in their own lives. Many rededicated their lives to Christ that day, realizing theyhad been choosingtheirOWN way instead of THE Way.

* * * * * * * * *

Think about it. **As those women walked on in hope and joy to spread the Good News,** the soldiers went to the priests, who went to the leaders, who bribed the soldiers, who went back to the people with....options.

And still those women walked on.

How could they squelch this Good News? Why, it would eternally alter the way things had always been! Things would never be the same! If people really BELIEVED that God had raised Jesus from the dead, why, who knew what could happen?

...and the women kept walking.

Are we walking with them?
Or are we, like those soldiers, chief priests, and leaders, choosing our own human-centered options?

Walking.....

Consider how our lives would be had it not been for those women and countless other people like them who kept walking the Way of Christ.

There is hope - incredible Hope...on the Way.
What 'options' are YOU exercising today?

Walking.....

Reflections

How do you think the world would be different if those women (and many people like them) had not kept walking the Way of Christ?

What difference do you think those who choose to walk the way of Christ today are making in the world? Your city or town? Your family?

What "options" are you exercising in your life?

60

Hope-Full Life

Now the eleven disciples went to Galilee, to the mountain to which Jesus had directed them. **When they saw him, they worshiped him; but some doubted.** *And Jesus came and said to them,* **"All authority in heaven and on earth has been given to me.** **Go therefore and make disciples** *of all nations, baptizing them in the name of the Father and of the Son and of the Holy Spirit,* *and teaching them to obey everything that I have commanded you. And* **remember, I am with you always, to the end of the age."**

- Matthew 28: 16-20 (New Revised Standard Version)

Then the eleven disciples left for Galilee, going to the mountain where Jesus had told them to go. **When they saw him, they worshiped him-- but some of them still doubted!** *Jesus came and told his disciples,* **"I have been given complete authority in heaven and on earth.** **Therefore, go and make disciples** *of all the nations, baptizing them in the name of the Father and the Son and the Holy Spirit.* *Teach these new disciples to obey all the commands I have given you. And* **be sure of this: I am with you always, even to the end of the age."**

- Matthew 28: 16-20 (New Living Translation)

Meanwhile, the eleven disciples were on their way to Galilee, headed for the mountain Jesus had set for their reunion. **The moment they saw him they worshiped him. Some, though, held back, not sure about worship, about risking themselves totally.** *Jesus, undeterred, went right ahead and gave his charge:* **"God authorized and commanded me to commission you: Go out and train everyone you meet,** *far and near, in this way of life, marking them by baptism in the threefold name: Father, Son, and Holy Spirit. Then instruct them in the practice of all that I have commanded you.* **I'll be with you as you do this, day after day after day, right up to the end of the age."**

- Matthew 28: 16-20 (The Message Version)

* * * * * * * * * *

God blessed me with the opportunity to serve as chaplain to a church preschool for the summer one year. Well, to be perfectly honest, I didn't feel too blessed when I was asked (OK, assigned) to this ministry. "It'll be good for you. You'll get a new perspective on faith and ministry," my mentor assured me. *Alrighty then.*

I was resigned to my fate, you might say....until that first day at 'chapel time'. The young boys and girls came each morning to hear a Bible story and sing a song or two. So there I was, sitting on the steps in the sanctuary waiting as they paraded in, far more excited to see me than...well, you get the picture.

And the topics? First, baptism, specifically Jesus's baptism. **Second, His instruction for us to go share that with others.** We sang a song and I told these two Bible stories.

A small boy sprang to his feet, excitement written all over his face. I read his nametag as it zipped before my eyes (He was sitting a mere two feet in front of me) - Mark. "I'm ready!" he blurted out. **"Jesus is WAY cool, and I want to follow him. Can I be baptized right NOW?"**

Whoa, I thought. I didn't prepare for this! Thoughts scrambling, I almost missed the quiet (but persistent) tugging on my sleeve. 'Missy', her nametag read. "Missy?" I asked, hoping I looked a lot braver than I felt. **"Pastor, I've only got one question. Do I have to get WET to get baptized?"**

* * * * * * * * * *

As Jesus spoke to the disciples that day, note that they all saw, but some worshipped, and some doubted. **Jesus spoke to them ALL.** Not just the doubters. Not just the worshippers. ALL of them. He spoke to them all. **He called them all.**

Just like the group of preschoolers I met that morning. Just like your group of friends. Just like the people you work with. Just like....us.

To all the 'Mark's', Jesus says, "Yes! <u>Now</u> - let's GO!"
And to all the 'Missy's', He says, "Yes! <u>Now</u>, and yes, you'll have to get wet!"

As we finish this walk through the Gospel of Matthew together, know that Jesus calls you and I just as surely as he called those disciples. He calls us just as surely as He called those preschoolers that day in the chapel.

There will be days when we'll say, "I'm ready! Jesus is cool, and I want to follow Him!".
But there will also be days when we too will answer, "Do I have to get wet?"

I pray that you'll find and live a hope-filled, hope-full life, showing all who meet you that you truly believe Jesus when He says, *I'll be with you as you do this, day after day after day, right up to the end of the age."*

Reflections

Why do people hesitate to "get wet" for Jesus, to totally immerse themselves in Christ-like living?

Why do people balk at the command to "Go!" and "Instruct" others about the Good News of Christ?

Which so you most identify with: Mark? Holly? Someone on the edges, watching and listening?

Appendix 1

Bible Translations and How to Find Them

Four versions/translations of Scripture are used in the Exploring... Bible study series. One or more of them may have appealed to you as you read and experienced this book. You may wonder what's different about them. You may have decided you'd like to purchase one or more.

The information contained here should assist you in doing just that. Here is a brief description of each version/ translation along with sources, should you decide to purchase one or more of them.

Contemporary English Version, published by the American Bible Society (ABS) in 1995, is available through them (www.bibles.com). Originally intended as a children's translation, it uses very simple, contemporary language which can be read and easily understood by those of all ages. The CEV is one of the versions recommended especially for those for whom English is a second language. The New Testament was translated directly from the Greek text; Psalms and Proverbs from the Masoretic Hebrew text; and the balance from their original languages as well.

New Revised Standard Version, published in 1989 by the National Council of Churches, is an updated version of the Revised Standard Version. The NRSV is available in most Christian and large volume bookstores, as well as from the American Bible Society (www.bibles.com). It is the most widely used ecumenical (used by many Christian traditions) version and is used in many seminaries. A committee of about thirty members of various Protestant denominations and the Roman Catholic Church participated, as well as Jewish and Eastern Orthodox participants for the Old Testament.

New Living Translation, published by Tyndale House Publishers in 1996, is available from many sources, which include Christian bookstores, large 'regular' bookstores, and online resources such as the American Bible Society (www.bibles.com). Bible Gateway (www.biblegateway.com) describes the NLT this way: "The goal of any Bible translation is to convey the meaning of the ancient Greek and Hebrew texts as accurately as possible to the modern reader. The New Living translation is based on the most recent scholarship in the theory of translation. The challenge for the translators was to create a text that would make the same impact in the life of modern readers that the original text had for the original readers. In the New Living Translation, this is accomplished by translating entire thoughts (rather than just words) into natural, everyday English. The end result is a translation that is easy to read and understand and that accurately communicates the meaning of the original text."

The Message, published by NavPress / Eugene Peterson, can be obtained at many Christian bookstores as well as 'regular' large bookstores. The Message can also be ordered through its own website: www.messagebible. com. It is described by the publisher as follows: "Why was *The Message* written? The best answer to that question comes from Eugene Peterson himself: 'While I was teaching a class on Galatians, I began to realize that the adults in my class weren't feeling the vitality and directness that I sensed as I read and studied the New Testament in its original Greek. Writing straight from the original text, I began to attempt to bring into English the rhythms and idioms of the original language. I knew that the early readers of the New Testament were captured and engaged by these writings and I wanted my congregation to be impacted in the same way. I hoped to bring the New Testament to life for two different types of people: those who hadn't read the Bible because it seemed too distant and irrelevant and those who had read the Bible so much that it had become 'old hat.'

"Peterson's parishioners simply weren't connecting with the real meaning of the words and the relevance of the New Testament for their own lives. So he began to bring into English the rhythms and idioms of the original ancient Greek—writing straight out of the Greek text without looking at other English translations. As he shared his version of Galatians with them, they quit stirring their coffee and started catching Paul's passion and excitement as he wrote to a group of Christians whom he was guiding in the ways of Jesus Christ. For more than two years, Peterson devoted all his efforts to *The Message New Testament*. His primary goal was to capture the tone of the text and the original conversational feel of the Greek, in contemporary English.

"Some people like to read the Bible in Elizabethan English. Others want to read a version that gives a close word-for-word correspondence between the original languages and English. Eugene Peterson recognized that the original sentence structure is very different from that of contemporary English. He decided to strive for the spirit of the original manuscripts—to express the rhythm of the voices, the flavor of the idiomatic expressions, the subtle connotations of meaning that are often lost in English translations.

"The goal of *The Message* is to engage people in the reading process and help them understand what they read. This is not a study Bible, but rather "a reading Bible." The verse numbers, which are not in the original documents, have been left out of the print version to facilitate easy and enjoyable reading. The original books of the Bible were not written in formal language. The Message tries to recapture the Word in the words we use today."

Appendix 2

Notes

All stories contained in this book are true. Names and identifying characteristics have been altered, except where persons have given permission to be identified.

Chapter 6

"American Dream", as sung by Casting Crowns. Hector Cervantes and Mark Hall, SWECS Music / Club Zoo Music.

Chapter 12

"He Lives!", words and music by Alfred H. Ackley, 1933.

Chapter 16

"When We All Get to Heaven", also called "Sing the Wondrous Love of Jesus", Emily D. Wilson and Eliza Hewitt, 1898.

Chapter 23

"Come Thou Long Expected Jesus", Charles Wesley, 1744.

About the author

Rev. Dr. Al W. Adams is an ordained pastor in the Christian Church (Disciples of Christ) tradition. She has served in many and varied locations and ministries, which have included hospital and police chaplaincy, congregational leadership, and church planting. Trained in coaching and mediation, she has also served as consultant, mentor, and seminar leader/facilitator for clergy, congregations, and leadership teams. Her passion is bringing individuals and congregations together as Scripture and faith come alive in them, thus enabling them to be and do more than they dare ask...or imagine! (Eph. 3:21) Dr. Al has a BS in Education and a Masters degree in counseling from the University of Missouri, a Masters of Divinity (M.Div.) from Eden Theological Seminary in St. Louis, and a Doctor of Ministry (D.Min.) from Brite Divinity School (Texas Christian University). This is the first book in the 'Exploring...Everyday Stories' series of Bible studies and preaching stories.

The *Exploring...* series is greeted with anticipation. The thoughtful, challenging and contemporary "ponderings" provide a meaningful opportunity to step outside the mundane activities of the everyday world and remind us to contemplate our relationships with one another and with God.

     Susan Burney (retired educator, author)

     John Burney (retired educator, currently head of Elders, Webster Groves Christian Church)

I am an old Christian but a new Christian in study of the Bible. Pastor Al has given me new insight into the message the Bible gives to each of us. I LOVE her stories. They speak to my heart, and they provide wonderful images for my mind to mull over. I have a new way to start my prayers with God. As one of the stories says, "Hello Love"- I know God smiles.

     Sue Aggson, member, United Methodist Church, Fort Morgan, CO

www.ingramcontent.com/pod-product-compliance
Lightning Source LLC
Chambersburg PA
CBHW062042090426

42740CB00016B/2987